OUT & ABOUT

• WALKING GUIDES TO BRITAIN •

No 7

The North of England

First published in Great Britain in 1996 by
Marshall Cavendish Books, London
(a division of Marshall Cavendish Partworks Ltd)

Copyright © 1996 Marshall Cavendish

ISBN 0319 00745 6

British Library Cataloguing in Publication Data:
A catalogue record for this book is available from the British Library

Printed and bound in Malaysia

Some of this material has previously appeared in the Marshall Cavendish partwork OUT & ABOUT

While every effort has been made to check the accuracy of these walks, neither Marshall Cavendish nor Ordnance Survey can be held responsible for any errors or omissions, nor for any consequences arising from the use of information contained in this book. Marshall Cavendish welcomes readers' letters pointing out changes that have taken place in land ownership, access, etc., or inaccuracies in the walks' routes or descriptions.

CONTENTS

Introduction to

OUT & ABOUT

• WALKING GUIDES TO BRITAIN •

Walking has become one of the most popular pastimes in Britain. To enjoy walking, you don't need any special skills, you don't have to follow rules or join expensive clubs, and you don't need any special equipment – though a pair of walking boots is a good idea! It is an easy way of relaxing and getting some exercise, and of enjoying nature and the changing seasons.

The OUT & ABOUT WALKING GUIDES TO BRITAIN will give you ideas for walks in your own neighbourhood and in other areas of Britain. All the walks are devised around a theme and range in length from about 2 to 9 miles (3.25 to 14.5 km) and in difficulty from very easy to mildly strenuous. Since each walk is circular, you will always be able to get back to your starting point.

Devised by experts and tested for accuracy, all the walks are accompanied by clear, practical instructions and an enlarged section of the relevant Ordnance Survey map. The flavour of the walk and highlights to look out for are described in the introductory text.

LOCAL COLOUR

Background features give you extra insight into items of local interest. The OUT & ABOUT WALKING GUIDES TO BRITAIN relate legends, point out unusual architectural details, provide a potted history of the lives of famous writers and artists connected with a particular place, explain traditional crafts still practised by local artisans, and uncover the secrets behind an ever-changing landscape.

DISCOVER NATURE

One of the greatest pleasures in going for a walk is the sense of being close to nature. On the walks suggested in the OUT & ABOUT WALKING GUIDES TO BRITAIN, you can feel the wind, smell the pine trees, hear the birds and see the beauty of the countryside. You will become more aware of the seasons – the life cycles of butterflies, the mating calls of birds, the protective behaviour of all creatures with their young. You will see the beginning of new life in the forests and fields, the bluebell carpets in spring woodlands, the dazzling beauty of rhododendron bushes in early summer, the swaying cornfields of summer and the golden colours of leaves in autumn. The OUT & ABOUT WALKING GUIDES TO BRITAIN tell you what to look out for and where to find it.

NATURE WALK

Occasional nature walk panels will highlight an interesting feature that you will see on your walk. You will learn about natural and manmade details in the landscape, how to tell which animal or bird has nibbled the cones in a pine forest, what nurse trees are and what a triangulation point is.

FACT FILE

The fact file will give you at-a-glance information about each walk to help you make your selection.

⊛ **general location**

os **map reference for Ordnance Survey map with grid reference for starting point**

miles 0 1 2 3 4 5 6 7 8 9
kms 0 1 2 3 4 5 6 7 8 9 10 11 12 13 14 15
length of the walk in miles and kilometres

◔ **time needed if walking at an average speed**

▬ **character of the walk: easy/easy with**

◼ **strenuous parts/mildly strenuous; hills to**

⬕ **be climbed and muddy or dangerous areas are pointed out**

P **parking facilities near the start of the walk**

T **public transport information**

🏛 **facilities for refreshment, including pubs**

🍴 **serving lunchtime meals, restaurants, tea rooms and picnic areas**

wc **location of toilets**

⌐ **historic sites**

ORDNANCE SURVEY MAPS

All the walks in the OUT & ABOUT WALKING GUIDES TO BRITAIN are illustrated on large-scale, full-colour maps supplied by the Ordnance Survey. Ordnance Survey are justifiably proud of their worldwide reputation for excellence and accuracy. For extra clarity, the maps have been enlarged to a scale of 1:21,120 (3 inches to 1 mile).

The route for each walk is marked clearly on the map with a broken red line, and the numbers along the

ABOVE: *Colourful narrowboats are always an attractive feature on inland waterways.*

route refer you to the numbered stages in the written directions. In addition, points of interest are marked on the maps with letters. Each one is mentioned in the walk directions and is described in detail in the introductory text.

COUNTRYWISE

The countryside is one of our greatest resources. If we treat it with respect, we can preserve it for the future.

Throughout the countryside there is a network of paths and byways. Some are former trading routes, others are simply the paths villagers took to visit one another in the days before public transport. Most are designated 'rights of way': footpaths, open only to people on foot, and bridleways, open to people on foot, horseback or bicycle. These paths can be identified on Ordnance Survey maps and verified, in cases of dispute, by the definitive map for the area, held by the relevant local authority.

THE LAW OF TRESPASS

If you find a public right of way barred to you, you may remove the obstruction or take a short detour around it. However, in England and Wales, if you stray from the footpath you are trespassing and could be sued in a civil court for damages. In Scotland, rights of way are not recorded on definitive maps, nor is there a law of trespass. Although you may cross mountain and moorland paths, landowners are permitted to impose restrictions on access, such as during the grouse-shooting season, which should be obeyed.

If you are following a public right of way and find, for example, that your path is blocked by a field of crops, you are entitled to walk the line of the footpath through the crops, in single file. Farmers are required, by law, to restore public rights of way within 14 days of ploughing. However, if you feel uncomfortable about doing this and can find a way round, then do so. But report the matter to the local authority who will take the necessary action to clear the correct route.

RIGHT: *The stunning patchwork of fields surrounding the picturesque village of Widecombe in the heart of Dartmoor makes a beautiful setting for the famous annual fair.*
BELOW: *Brown hares boxing in spring are a fascinating sight.*

It is illegal for farmers to place a bull on its own in a field crossed by a right of way (unless the bull is not a recognized dairy breed). If you come across a bull alone in a field, find another way round.

COMMONS AND PARKS

There are certain areas in England and Wales where you may be able to wander without keeping to paths, such as most commons and beaches. There are also country parks, set up by local authorities for public recreation – parkland, woodland, heath or farmland.

The National Trust is the largest private landowner in England and Wales. Its purpose is to preserve areas of natural beauty and sites of historic interest by acquisition, holding them in trust for public access and enjoyment. Information on access may be obtained from National Trust headquarters at

THE COUNTRY CODE

■ **Enjoy the countryside, and respect its life and work**

■ **Always guard against risk of fire**

■ **Fasten all gates**

■ **Keep your dogs under close control**

■ **Keep to public footpaths across farmland**

■ **Use gates and stiles to cross fences, hedges and walls**

■ **Leave livestock, crops and machinery alone**

■ **Take your litter home**

■ **Help to keep all water clean**

■ **Protect wildlife, plants and trees**

■ **Take special care on country roads**

■ **Make no unnecessary noise**

ABOVE RIGHT *Carelessness with cigarettes, matches or camp fires can be devastating in a forest.*

36 QueenAnne's Gate, London SW1H 9AS
Tel: 0171-222 9251.

Most regions of great scenic beauty in England and Wales are designated National Parks or Areas of Outstanding Natural Beauty (AONB). In Scotland, they are known as National Scenic Areas (NSAs) or AONBs.

Most of this land is privately owned and there is no right of public access. In some cases, local authorities may have negotiated agreements with landowners to allow walkers access on mountains and moors.

CONSERVATION

National park, AONB or NSA status is intended to provide some measure of protection for the land-scape, guarding against unsuitable development while encouraging enjoyment of its natural beauty.

Nature reserves are areas set aside for conservation. Most are privately owned, some by large organizations such as the Royal Society for the Protection of Birds. Although some offer public access, most require permission to enter.

THE RAMBLERS ASSOCIATION

The aims of the Ramblers Association are to further greater understanding and care of the countryside, to protect and enhance public rights of way and areas of natural beauty, to improve public access to the countryside, and to encourage more people to take up rambling as a healthy, recreational activity. It has played an important role in preserving and developing our national footpath network.

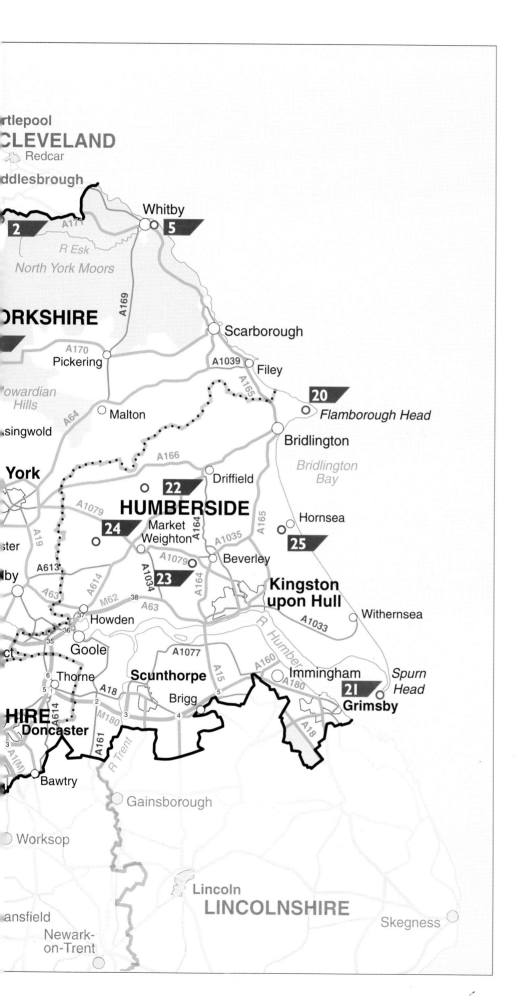

The North of England

All the walks featured in this book are plotted and numbered on the regional map (left) and listed in the box below.

USING MAPS

Although the OUT & ABOUT WALKING GUIDES TO BRITAIN give you all the information you need, it is useful to have some basic map skills. Most of us have some experience of using a motoring atlas to navigate by car. Navigating when walking is much the same, except that mistakes are much more time and energy consuming and, if circumstances conspire, could lead to an accident.

A large-scale map is the answer to identifying where you are. Britain is fortunate in having the best mapping agency in the world, the Ordnance Survey, which produces high-quality maps, the most popular being the 1:50,000 Landranger series. However, the most useful for walkers are the 1:25,000 Pathfinder, Explorer and Outdoor Leisure maps.

THE LIE OF THE LAND

A map provides more than just a bird's eye view of the land; it also conveys information about the terrain – whether marshy, forested, covered with tussocky grass or boulders; it distinguishes between footpaths and bridleways; and shows boundaries such as parish and county boundaries.

Symbols are used to identify a variety of landmarks such as churches, camp and caravan sites, bus, coach and rail stations, castles, caves and historic houses. Perhaps most importantly of all, the shape of the land is indicated by contour lines. Each line represents land at a specific height so it is possible to read the gradient from the spacing of the lines (the closer the spacing, the steeper the hill).

GRID REFERENCES

All Ordnance Survey maps are over-printed with a framework of squares known as the National Grid. This is a reference system which, by breaking the country down into squares, allows you to pinpoint any place in the country and give it a unique reference number; very useful when making rendezvous arrangements. On OS Landranger, Pathfinder and Outdoor Leisure maps it is possible to give a reference to an accuarcy of 100 metres. Grid squares on these maps cover an area of 1 km x 1 km on the ground.

GIVING A GRID REFERENCE

Blenheim Palace in Oxfordshire has a grid reference of **SP 441 161.** This is constructed as follows:

  SP These letters identify the 100 km grid square in which Blenheim Palace lies. These squares form the basis of the National Grid. Information on the 100 km square covering a particular map is always given in the map key.

  441 161 This six figure reference locates the position of Blenheim Palace to 100 metres in the 100 km grid square.

  44 This part of the reference is the number of the grid line which forms the western (left-hand) boundary of the 1 km grid square in which Blenheim Palace appears. This number is printed in the top and bottom margins of the relevant OS map (Pathfinder 1092 in this case).

  16 This part of the reference is the number of the grid line which forms the southern (lower) boundary of the 1 km grid square in which Blenheim Palace appears. This number is printed in the left- and right-hand margins of the relevant OS map (Pathfinder 1092).

  These two numbers together (SP 4416) locate the bottom left-hand corner of the 1 km grid square in which Blenheim Palace appears. The remaining figures in the reference **441 161** pinpoint the position within that square by dividing its western boundary lines into tenths and estimating on which imaginary tenths line Blenheim Palace lies.

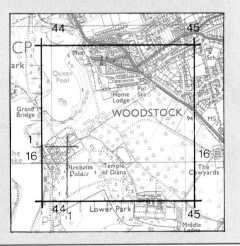

A WALK IN WHARFEDALE

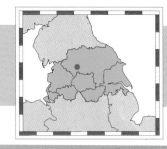

Through the dramatic limestone landscape of the Dales

Set in the beautiful Yorkshire Dales National Park, this walk through part of Upper Wharfedale includes spectacular views of the Dales countryside, and takes in the villages of Grassington and Linton.

Between the two villages is St Michael's Church, Linton **C**, one of the finest churches in the Dales. It has a bell turret but no tower, and stands on what was almost certainly an Anglo-Saxon, possibly even a pagan, site, which explains its distance from the four village communities it originally served: Grassington, Linton, Threshfield and Hebden. The stepping stones over the River Wharfe formed part of the ancient Parishioners' Way to Hebden village until its own church was built in the last century.

THE SNAKE WALK

Grassington **A**, where the walk begins, is a former leadmining village with an attractive cobbled square. From here the walk follows a winding footpath with high walls, known as the Snake Walk, which was used by millworkers to and from Linton Mill. Now replaced by cottages, this former textile mill was powered by a weir upstream. Nearby Linton falls **B** is a natural limestone feature where acrobatic swallows and low-flying dippers are frequent visitors.

AN IDYLLIC VILLAGE

Linton village **D** is set around a beautiful green overlooked by a

▲ *Linton Falls, where the dipper (inset), an underwater swimmer, can be seen.*
▼ *St Michael's is a 12th-century church.*

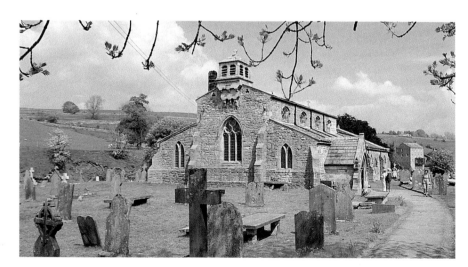

FACT FILE

⚹ Grassington, Yorkshire Dales National Park on the B6265 Skipton–Pateley road

▭ Outdoor Leisure Map 10, grid reference SE 003638

◔ Allow 2 hours

▬ Field paths with three uphill sections; several steep stiles, some with ladder-like steps

P National Park Centre car park, Hebden Road, Grassington

T Keighley and District bus services from Skipton. Dalesbus services from Leeds, Bradford and Ilkley daily

▦ Refreshments at hotels and pubs in Grassington and Linton

WC At car park and between Linton Mill and St Michael's Church

THE WALK

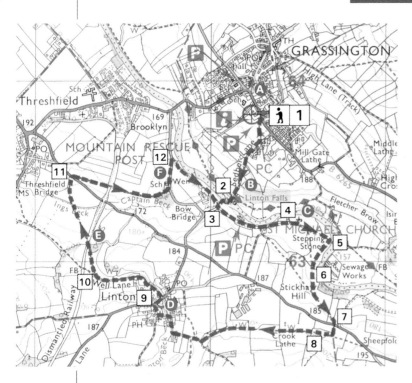

hand side of the churchyard to another stile. Keep straight on to river.

5 Do not go over the stepping stones. Instead, turn right, make for the wall ahead and climb ladder stile.

6 Climb the hillside along a faint path heading above the fir plantation on the left. As you reach the brow of the hill, make for the narrow stile in the centre of the wall on the left. Cross the next field to a second stile and make for a stile by the gate which leads into the road.

7 Turn right for 16 yards (15 metres) along the road and go through the gate on the left into a field. The path goes up alongside the wall at the field's edge and around the corner to a stone step stile on the right.

8 Cross the next field to another stile and keep to the right of the barn ahead. Continue over two more stiles and alongside a wall for about 400 yards (360 metres) to a stile which leads on to a farm track. Turn right into Linton **D**,

crossing the stream by the footbridge to the Green.

9 Leave the village in the Grassington direction, but then turn left along the track signposted to Threshfield, which runs alongside the stream.

10 At the gate, bear right to the underpass below the old railway line **E** and through the gates. Follow the path to a slab bridge over the stream, climb the stile and continue up past a wood to the wall corner at the road.

11 Cross the road and bear slightly right to the gate and a grassy path that leads to a gated bridge over the old railway and a track down to Threshfield School **F**. Turn left into lane and walk past the school.

12 About 160 yards (150 metres) past the school look for a narrow gap stile on the right, which leads to a narrow riverside path past a weir. Continue to a little packhorse bridge and the wooden bridge at Linton Falls. Turn left and walk back uphill to Grassington.

GRASSINGTON-LINTON

The walk begins in the National Park car park, Grassington **A**.

1 Leave the car park by the kissing gate in the bottom left-hand corner. Turn right down the enclosed, winding footpath to Linton Falls **B**.

2 Cross the new wooden footbridge over the waterfalls, turning right to a junction of paths where you turn left into a lane by some new cottages.

3 Walk along the lane towards Linton Church **C**.

4 The path goes via a step stile at the side of the church gate, and along the right-

black and white pub, and is perhaps the least spoiled of all the Dales villages. Most of the houses date from the 17th and 18th centuries. Fountain's Hospital, an almshouse for 'six poor men or women of the parish' was endowed by a local man, Richard Fountain, in 1721.

The legend of Threshfield School **F** tells of a ghostly figure, Pam the Fiddler, who haunts the schoolroom at night playing the fiddle with demonic power. At one time the Yorkshire Dales Railway **E** carried hundreds of tourists between Skipton and Grassington, but now only the trackbed remains.

◄ *Narrow streets characteristic of Grassington. (right) One of the four bridges crossing the beck in Linton.*

A VOYAGE OF DISCOVERY

Through the countryside where Captain Cook spent his childhood

This walk through scenic North Yorkshire Countryside connects five places associated with the early life of Captain James Cook. Despite obvious changes, some features are essentially the same as when he knew them. The farm where he lived for eight years still nestles at the foot of the moor; All Saints' churchyard **C** in Great Ayton contains the grave of his brothers and sisters, and the school where he was educated is also there, although it now houses a collection of Cook memorabilia. The walk also offers spectacular views across the Cleveland Plain to the

FACT FILE

- ⚹ Great Ayton, 5 miles (8 km) from Guisborough

- Pathfinder 601 (NZ41/51), grid reference NZ 591110

  miles 0 1 2 3 4 5 6 7 8 9 10 miles
  kms 0 1 2 3 4 5 6 7 8 9 10 11 12 13 14 15 kms

- ◔ Allow 4 ½ hours

- Gradual ascent to Easby Moor, but steep descent through a wood. There is a steady climb through a wood towards Airy Holme Farm

- **P** Gribdale Gate car park, 2 miles (3.2 km) east of Great Ayton

- Inns, cafés, shops in Great Ayton

- **WC** By the Captain Cook Schoolroom Museum

▲ *The spectacular Roseberry Topping dominates the flat expanse of Great Ayton Moor. (inset) The wren is a frequent visitor here. (below) Cook learned the three Rs at Great Ayton village school — his education was paid for by his father's employer, Thomas Scottowe.*

LITTLE AYTON — GREAT AYTON

The walk begins at Gribdale Gate car park.

1 From the cattle grid take the signposted Cleveland Way path into Cleveland Forest. Pass through a wooden gate and walk up the broad track between conifers. Steps lead up to the heather-covered top of Easby Moor and to the Captain Cook monument **A**. Take in the wide-ranging view **B**.

2 With your back to the inscription on the monument, look to the right and notice two stone gateposts at about 100 yards (90 metres). Pass through the posts on to a well-worn track. On the left you pass a small quarry where the stones for the monument were cut. The path continues steeply down, with a broken-down wall on your left. At the end of this wall the distinct path splits; take the right fork which descends

through the conifers. This track descends to a forestry road where you should turn left and continue for about 250 yards (225 metres). Follow the road round a sharp right bend and proceed for another 250 yards (225 metres), passing through a gate to a wall corner 50 yards (45 metres) beyond.

3 From the wall corner go straight along on a well-used path, following the top edge of the field to a gate, which leads into a grassy lane with a wire fence on either side. The grassy lane eventually becomes a tarmac road and 70 yards (63 metres) after this point turn left through a gate signposted 'Fir-brook'.

4 The farm lane passes through metal gates, over the Whitby - Middlesbrough railway line and descends into Little Ayton, passing to the right of the buildings at Brookside Farm.

5 At the road junction turn right, away from the

THE WALK

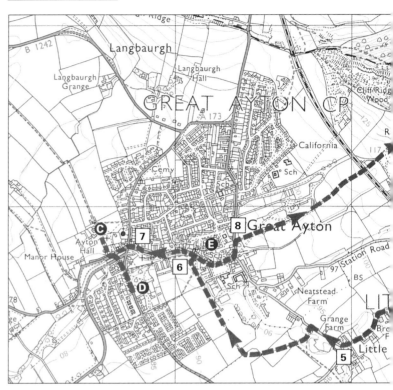

metal bridge. At the far end of the first house on the left, turn left along a signposted path to a footbridge. Bear right across the field on a poorly marked path and bear right again on the path across the next field to a stile

beside a gate. Continue on the distinct path across the field. This path then follows the hedge on your right past a sports field. Stiles and a gate lead to a footbridge over the River Leven into Great Ayton.

6 Turn left along the

hills which form the north-western edge of the North York Moors. The county of Cleveland is due north.

A YORKSHIRE BOYHOOD

From viewpoint **B** the panorama includes the village of Marton,

▲ *The charming graveyard at All Saints' Church in Great Ayton is the final resting place of several members of Cook's family.*

◄ *The stone cottage that Cook's father built in Great Ayton was moved brick by brick to Australia and now stands in Fitzroy Gardens, Melbourne.*

where Cook was born. The site of his birthplace is set in a park and an excellent museum is nearby. Two miles (3.2 km) to the north-west is Great Ayton. Across the plain to the south-west are the Cleveland Hills, rising to nearly 1500 feet (450 metres) above sea level. From right to left they are Carlton Bank, Cringle Moor, Cold Moor and Hasty Bank, with Urra Moor the highest point on the North York Moors to the south. To the north is the peak of Roseberry Topping and Great Ayton Moor.

Cook was educated, probably until he was 12, at the Michael Postgate school. It is likely that he learned to read at a dame school at Marton where he added writing and arithmetic to the skills which he put to such good use in later life. An outside staircase at the back leads to the upper storey where there is the

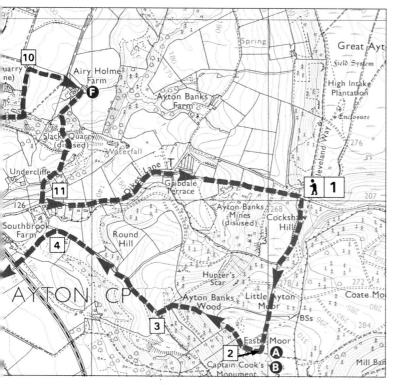

Continue on the left past the Royal Oak pub, bear left at the road junction along the main road and in a 100 yards (90 metres) turn right through a metal kissing gate set in a wall.

8 The path leads to another kissing gate, then a series of gates lead through a copse and in a straight line across parkland to the railway line. Look out for trains, then cross the railway and continue to a junction of tracks. Cross the stile opposite and continue with the wire fence on your left. Follow the fence to the left and cross the stile into a wood.

9 The path climbs to a junction; turn right, then immediately left and continue climbing through the oak and beech wood. Near the top there are fine views across the Cleveland Plain, with Great Ayton below. Cross a stile into a field and turn left, keeping the wire fence on your left, to

another stile. Turn right, away from the stile, along the top of the field. Roseberry Topping lies straight ahead and Airy Holme Farm is below. Cross the stile and continue with a wire fence on the right to a stile.

10 Cross the stile, turn right and descend to Airy Holme Farm **F**. At the junction of tracks go straight ahead, passing to the left of the farm buildings. Join a road passing through a wood and on to a junction.

11 Turn left along the road for 1/2 mile (800 metres). The road turns sharp left at a telephone box but continue straight ahead on a track behind the houses. At the end of the terrace bear right to a stile through the hedge, turn left and keeping the wire fence on your left climb to a stile beside a gate. Continue straight ahead to a metal gate on your left. Turn left then right along the fence back to the car park .

High Street to the road junction beside the bridge.

7 Walk down the road opposite (Low Green) and take the second road on the right to All Saints' Church **C**. Retrace your steps, cross over the bridge and walk straight ahead along

the road to an obelisk in a small garden on your left. This was the site of Captain Cook's father's cottage **D**. Return to **7** and retrace your steps down the High Street. Just beyond the bridge is the Captain Cook Schoolroom Museum **E**.

small, but interesting, Captain Cook Schoolroom Museum **E**.

Airy Holme Farm **F** became the family home in 1735. Sheep and cattle would have grazed the steeper pastures while crops would have been grown in the more level fields that could be ploughed.

In 1755 James Cook senior built a cottage in Great Ayton. The custom in this area is for the owners to incorporate their initials in the stone above the doorway. The cottage carries the inscription 'J, G' with a 'C' above for James and Grace Cook.

LINKS WITH AUSTRALIA

The site of the cottage **D** is now marked by an obelisk. The cottage

Airy Holme Farm was Cook's home until he was apprenticed as a haberdasher at the age of 17.

Captain James Cook
R.N., F.R.S.

James Cook (1728-79) rose from humble beginnings to become the greatest seaman of his time. He became an apprentice on a collier transporting coal to and from Whitby and it was a Whitby ship that he chose to take on his three great voyages of exploration.

During these voyages he dispelled the myth of the existence of a great southern continent. He accurately charted and explored the whole coastline of New Zealand and the east coast of Australia and was the first navigator to explore the Antarctic region. On his final voyage he searched for the North West Passage between the Pacific and Atlantic Oceans across northern Canada.

James Cook was an excellent administrator, planner and manager of seafarers.

Cook first came to the Navy's attention when his survey of the St Lawrence river in Canada enabled British forces to capture Louisberg and Quebec from the French. But on his first great voyage of exploration it was as an astronomer that he was sent to Tahiti to observe the transit of Venus across the sun. He also experimented successfully with combating scurvy among sailors by the use of fresh vegetables and fruit juice. His paper on the subject won him the Royal Society Gold Medal.

During most of his time in the Pacific, Cook maintained good relations with the local people, but during a confrontation after the theft of a boat on Hawaii, he was killed. He was mourned not only by his crew but by the people of Hawaii, who gave him a chief's funeral.

the blocks in time to meet a steamer which called four times a year at the nearby lighthouse. The 39 granite blocks were transferred successfully to the boat from the rocky coastline having been dragged there by four horses. The following morning the steamer *Cape York* with the stones on board hove to at the exact place where the *Endeavour* first sighted the

◀ *The peaceful river running through Great Ayton may have inspired Cook's nautical leanings. (below) The Cook Monument on Easby Moor.*

Australian coast and the blocks were shipped to Great Ayton.

Easby Monument **A** was erected by Robert Campion of Easby Hall. The foundation stone was laid on 12th July 1827, 51 years after Cook left Plymouth on his third great voyage. On 27th October 1828, the centenary of Cook's birth, the top stone was laid in place by Robert Campion's son. The intention was for the monument to be 40 feet (12 metres) high so that it would be visible from the sea. Its actual height is 51 feet (15 metres).

itself was moved to Fitzroy Gardens, Melbourne and re-erected in 1934 as part of the state's centenary celebrations. It was taken down brick by brick, each one numbered, and placed in 253 packing cases. Even the creeper growing along the side of the house was shipped to Melbourne! The cottage is now one of Australia's top tourist attractions.

LAND AHOY!

The stones which form the obelisk are from Point Hicks Hill in Victoria, which was named by Captain Cook after Lieutenant Zachary Hicks who first sighted the Australian coast on Cook's first voyage. This remote headland is 26 miles (41.6 km) from the nearest settlement. A team of stonemasons went overland and cut

VIEW FROM THE TOP

Walking around the rugged Sutton Bank escarpment

Sutton Bank is undeniably one of the most popular beauty spots in Yorkshire. From the top of the escarpment you can see Gormire Lake **F**, which glistens like a jewel. Westward, across the Vales of York and Mowbray, there is a panoramic view of the Yorkshire Dales.

THE CLEVELAND WAY

This circular walk leads through open farmland and around an extensive area of grassland gallops used for training racehorses. The return to the steep escarpment of Sutton Bank follows part of the Cleveland Way, which is one of the Countryside Commission's designated national trails.

FACT FILE

✳ Sutton Bank, 5 miles (8 km) east of Thirsk on the A170

▱ Outdoor Leisure Map 26, grid reference SE 516830

miles 0 1 2 3 4 5 6 7 8 9 10 miles
kms 0 1 2 3 4 5 6 7 8 9 10 11 12 13 14 15 kms

◔ Allow 1¾ hours

▭ Mostly level walking. Not suitable for pushchairs and you should take care of children at roadside and escarpment edges. Can be muddy

P Free public car parks at the top of Sutton Bank

🍴 Sutton Bank has a café and picnic places. The Hambleton Inn is nearby. Toilets are WC alongside the eastern car park

▲*Sutton Bank is a high viewpoint for Gormire Lake, the Vale of York and the Pennines. The great tit (inset) is common throughout Britain and can be spotted in all seasons.*

The skies above Sutton Bank are often busy with gliders that soar overhead on strong up-currents and rising pockets of warm air. The Yorkshire Gliding Club, established in 1931, has its station and airfield on the remarkably flat stretch of land above the sweeping semi-circle of very steep cliffs. This natural amphitheatre creates thermals and also funnels the prevailing westerly winds into strong up-currents.

The flat limestone lands of the Hambleton Hills around Sutton Bank provide suitable conditions for horse racing. The sport was well established as early as 1612 and racegoers would seek refreshment at the Hambleton Inn **A** and Dialstone

THE WALK

SUTTON BANK

The walk starts from the eastern car park at the top of Sutton Bank. An information centre is situated between the two car parks.

1 From the rear (eastern) car park, walk to the exit/entrance junction with the main road (A170). Turn left, signposted Scarborough, and walk along the roadside grass verge.

2 Walk along the front edge of the Hambleton Inn **A** car park, which then leads to a narrow lane, signposted Cleveland Way, running parallel with the main road. Follow this lane as it bends left and then enters a woodland area.

3 Continue ahead, past the driveway entrance to Hambleton House **B**. Beyond the driveway, the Cleveland Way turns right, but you should continue ahead. This part of the route follows an ancient highway **C**. Follow the signpost for Dialstone. The route leads through the

gap in the white wood fencing and over the bark-laid horse track. Follow the grass track ahead with the old limestone wall on your right. Cross the driveway entrance to Hambleton High House and continue ahead in the direction of the radio mast.

4 At the road junction, take the road signposted for Boltby and Hawnby. After 50 yards (45 metres) turn left and walk along the driveway to Dialstone

Farm **D**. As you approach the farm entrance, turn left following the public bridleway sign, with the fence rail of the horse gallops on your left.

5 Near the disused quarry, the track makes a double bend. Follow the sign for Jennett Well with the stone wall and quarry on your left.

6 Bear right past the group of wind-blown Scots pines and over the stile to

turn left along the escarpment edge. As you start walking along the escarpment White Mare Crag **E** is on your right. You can enjoy the vista which includes Gormire Lake **F**.

7 Either return to the car park or make a short detour to cross the busy main road. Walk to the escarpment edge to see White Mare Crag and to enjoy the splendid panorama from this popular viewpoint.

Inn — now Dialstone Farm **D** — the name of which probably originates from the dial or weighing machine used to weigh in the jockeys. In 1755 the main prize 'The Hundred Guineas' was transferred to York and, as a result, the local races went into rapid decline. However, the tradition continues with the racing stables at Hambleton House **B** and the use of the gallops for training.

Gormire Lake is the only natural lake of any significant size in the North York Moors. Its formation dates from the end of the Ice Age, when part of a meltwater channel was blocked by a landslide at the escarpment edge. Local legends suggest that the lake is bottomless and that it is haunted by a white mare and its rider who plunged to their watery grave from the cliffs above. The 70 feet (21 metres) of vertical cliff face that rises above Gormire Lake is referred to as White Mare

◄*Hambleton House, with its racing stables and nearby gallops, lies at the foot of the Hambleton Hills.*

Cragg **E** or Whitestone Cliff.

After a rock-fall in 1755, the freshly revealed limestone face was said to have the appearance, from a distance, of a white horse. A nature trail circles the lake, which is a breeding place for wild duck, coot and sometimes the great crested grebe.

THE DROVE ROAD

Part of the walk follows a highway **C** that was used by Scottish cattlemen (drovers). In the 18th and 19th centuries they drove their cattle into England to sell meat to the expanding market and industrial towns. The 15-mile (24-km) of highway from Sutton Bank to Osmotherley is known as the Hambleton Drove Road and the weary drovers would have quenched their thirst at the Hambleton or Dialstone Inn.

HERRIOT COUNTRY

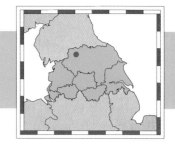

A gentle walk around the stone walls and lofty fells of the Dales

This is the countryside made famous by James Herriot in his series of books about the adventures of a Yorkshire vet. These were the basis of a film — then the long-running TV series — *All Creatures Great and Small*.

Despite the bluff scenery, the walk along the floor of Wensleydale is easy and links two contrasting villages. Bainbridge stands on a site inhabited since Roman times, the houses standing around the village green. Askrigg, which was once the main town in the valley, climbs past the church. Complementing the villages is the superb scenery of the Yorkshire Dales.

FORESTS OF WOLVES

The green at Bainbridge **A** is surrounded on three sides by stone cottages and at the northern end by the Rose and Crown Hotel. On the green is a set of stocks, once a warning to wrongdoers. Inside the Rose and Crown is a horn that is blown at nine o'clock each night between 27th September and Shrovetide, the

▲*The River Ure winds slowly through the majestic countryside of the Yorkshire dales. The dunlin (right) breeds in the Yorkshire dales and winters along the coast.*

▲*The stocks at Bainbridge no longer stand as a deterrent to wrongdoing, but as a reminder of a crueller age.*

three days before Ash Wednesday. The custom dates back to medieval times when Bainbridge was surrounded by forests where wolves roamed. The sounding of the horn in those days acted as a guide for travellers to reach the village safely.

CLOCKMAKERS

The stone houses of Askrigg **C** wind up the hillside. St Oswald's Church dates back to 1240 and the lead which covers the roof came from local mines. In front of the church, surrounded by cobbles, is the market cross, the charter of which was granted by Elizabeth I. In the 18th century the village was noted for its clockmakers. Incredibly, the grandfather clocks which were sold to people in Swaledale were carried over the 1,700-foot (510-metre) high

FACT FILE

- Bainbridge, 13 miles (20.8 km) west of Leyburn on the A684
- Outdoor Leisure Map 30, grid reference SD 933902

miles 0　1　2　3　4　5　6　7　8　9　10 miles
kms 0　1　2　3　4　5　6　7　8　9　10　11　12　13　14　15　kms

- Allow 2½ hours
- An easy walk with one climb after Worton
- **P** Street parking in Bainbridge
- **T** Bus service to Leyburn and Hawes
- Cafés, shops and inns in Bainbridge and Askrigg
- **WC** Toilets in Bainbridge

THE WALK

BAINBRIDGE – ASKRIGG

The walk begins at the green in Bainbridge **A**.

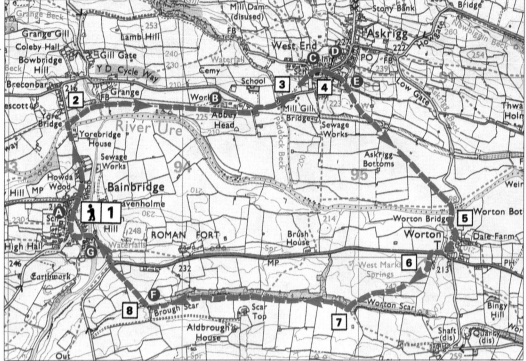

1 Take the road to the right of the Rose and Crown Hotel. Continue down the road and cross the bridge over the River Ure.

2 Turn right through a squeeze stile which is signposted 'Footpath to Askrigg'. Cross the field along a partially paved track to a footbridge. Note the small packhorse bridge upstream. Cross over a track, then go through a gate and continue with the former railway embankment on your left. Continue walking straight ahead until you pass the former Askrigg Railway Station buildings **B**. At the end of the field, turn left up the track to the road and then turn right for 200 yards (180 metres).

3 Turn left through a stile in the wall along a path signposted 'Askrigg ¼'. A paved path leads over two fields and then towards the church into Askrigg village **C**.

4 Across the road from the church entrance is 'Skeldale House' **D**. Take the lane below the house which is signposted 'FP Worton ¾'. After about 100 yards (90 metres), fork to the right and in about 50 yards (45 metres) there is a gate where you can pause for a fine view of the dale **E**. Pass through the small gate beside the field gate and keep the stone wall on your right. Follow the path that swings to the left over the field to a metal gate, then cross the former railway track in order to reach a metal gate. Two squeeze stiles lead to a paved path over the fields.

5 Turn right along the road crossing over the River Ure. Continue bearing right in Worton to the main road, then turn right. After 50 yards (45 metres) turn left and pass through the gate on the right signposted 'Bainbridge'.

6 Climb diagonally over the field to a fenced corner. Pass through a former gateway in a stone wall and head for a squeeze stile at the foot of a small valley. Then continue to the top of the small crag.

7 Turn right with a wall on your left. Keep children under control for the next ½ mile (800 metres) as the crag top is unfenced. Eventually pass through a gate and continue with the wall on your right. When you reach a belt of trees in front of you turn right through a squeeze stile. There is an excellent view of the Roman fort site **F**.

8 Descend with a wall on your left to a stile, then continue diagonally over the field to a squeeze stile 40 yards (36 metres) below the stone barn. Continue descending to the left of the pole to a stile onto a road. Turn right, then left, descending to the bridge over the River Bain **G** and back into the centre of Bainbridge.

▲*The partially paved footpath leads across the sheep pastures from Bainbridge to Askrigg.*

ridge by just two men. The clock mechanism was carried separately in a basket.

The tall stone house **D** opposite the church may seem familiar, for it has been used on numerous occasions as Skeldale House in the BBC TV series *All Creatures Great and Small*. After fund raising by the stars of the show, including a charity cricket match, the house was bought in 1979 as a residential home for elderly folk in the dale.

The dale **E** is famous for its cheese. The first Wensleydale cheeses were made in medieval times by the Cistercian monks at Jervaulx Abbey. At that time all the cheeses were pickled in brine, creating a finer-flavoured cheese.

Standing just to the east of Bainbridge is the site of the Roman fort of Virosidum **F**. It was built by Agricola and was occupied until the end of the 4th century AD. Roads radiated out from the fort to York, Lancaster, Ilkley and Stainmore.

Looking back over the bridge, upstream, there is a delightful view of a number of small waterfalls on the River Bain **G**. The river is the shortest in Britain, running about 2 miles (3.2 km) from its source at Semer Water to the River Ure.

WHITBY'S CLIFFS

This cliff-top walk begins from a town rich in history

From where the walk starts on the East Cliff at Whitby, there is a panoramic view of this ancient fishing port. The River Esk reaches the sea here through the confines of a steep-sided valley and twin headlands that face out to the North Sea. The fleet of sea-going vessels on the harbourside is protected from the fierce North Sea by the lengthy pincered piers.

TWO FAMOUS LANDMARKS

Across the river stand the famous headland landmarks of the whalebone gateway and Captain Cook's Monument ©. A very different architectural heritage lies below in the old town, with its jumble of red-pantiled roofs, offering indistinct and narrow gaps for the passage of

---

FACT FILE

* Whitby, 17 miles (27 km) north-west of Scarborough

* Outdoor Leisure Map 27, grid reference NZ 902113

  miles 0 1 2 3 4 5 6 7 8 9 10 miles
  kms 0 1 2 3 4 5 6 7 8 9 10 11 12 13 14 15 kms

* Allow 4 hours

* Coastal cliffs and town walk along harbourside and through the old part of the town

* **P** Near the abbey

* **T** Train to Middlesbrough. Buses to Scarborough, Pickering and Middlesbrough

* All facilities in Whitby

* **WC** At the car park

▶ *Whitby Abbey was founded by Saxons, destroyed by Danes, then re-founded by Benedictine monks c. 1070.*

▲*Whitby is built on both banks of the River Esk and is a busy fishing port and holiday resort. The black-headed gull (inset) has a harsh, rasping cry and eats anything from fish to refuse.*

human and commercial traffic.

A cliff path takes you along the route of the Cleveland Way, a National Trail which skirts the boundaries of the North York Moors National Park and extends south along the coast to Filey. The walk goes along the cliff edge as far as Gnipe Howe, when it turns inland

THE WALK

WHITBY

The walk starts from the Abbey Plain car park near to Whitby Abbey **A**.

1 Walk alongside the perimeter wall of the churchyard **B** of St Mary's to the cliff edge and turn right along the cliff path. On the opposite headland is Captain Cook's memorial **C**. The path leads you in front of the coastguard station **D** and a television mast and continues along a broad walk to Saltwick Holiday Park.

2 A path leads you into the holiday village,

following the Cleveland Way sign. Turn left along the tarmac road to continue past the shop and reception area. On leaving the holiday park, do not take the footpath signed to the beach, but continue ahead on the tarmac path and shortly branch off left to rejoin the cliff edge. The route takes you along the cliff side of the Fog Station **E** perimeter wall. Cross the next field diagonally up to the top corner, towards the lighthouse **F**.

3 Cross over the access road and turn left along a

path that skirts the perimeter wall of the lighthouse grounds. Continue ahead through the field. The path runs parallel with the cliff edge and eventually reaches a high point on the cliff. From here the trail keeps close company with the cliff edge.

4 The path dips down to cross a small gully and stream. Climb up the other side and along the cliff-line edge of the field. Carefully note the boundaries of the next two fields, to your right, at the end of which you will turn right.

5 Turn right over the stile, where there is a footpath sign to Hawsker,

and walk uphill with the field boundary on your right.

6 On reaching a field corner, bear right to cut across diagonally to the field gate. Go through the field gate and continue straight ahead on the track between the farm buildings. The track eventually takes a left turn.

7 At the junction of the farm tracks, turn right. Continue along here, past

the entrance to Widdy Field farm. Follow the track as it bears left to reach Whitby Laithes Farm.

8 Go through the gate at Whitby Laithes Farm and turn right along the track in front of the farmhouse.

9 At the end of the track, turn through the field gate on your right. Turn left where a bridleway is signposted and walk along the edge of the field with the fence line on your left. At the end of the field, turn left through the field gate and ahead to another field gate giving access to the tarmac lane.

10 Turn left along the tarmac lane, which is the access road for the lighthouse.

11 Go through the field gate and turn left along the lane between the farm buildings and through another field gate.

12 On reaching the main road, turn right. Take careful note as you pass the entrance to Knowles Farm (on the right). About 30 yards (27 metres) beyond it, turn off left down a narrow path.

13 Look carefully for a small break in the field boundary, on the left, just at the start of a small rise in the road. Turn left along this fenced path that soon leads past a high wall boundary. Go through the handgate and continue ahead with the farmhouse on your left, to join a tarmac lane. At a bend in the lane, keep to the left along a flagged path. On reaching the road, cross and walk along the footpath. Immediately in front of the road circle, turn left down the steep steps to reach the harbour road. Turn right to walk towards the town. The Penny Hedge ceremony takes place alongside the upper harbour **G** here.

14 At the bend in the road, cross straight over and walk along Church Street through the old town. At the end of the street, bear right to walk up the 199 steps to Caedmon's cross **H**, St Mary's Church and the Abbey Plain car park.

◀It was on the seas off the cliffs of Whitby that the young Captain Cook served his apprenticeship. Fields sweep up to the path (below) out of Whitby on one side, while on the other are rocky cliffs which drop to the sea.

through farmland and a country lane, eventually descending to Whitby's harbourside and a maze of narrow streets, yards and alleys through the old town.

A cacophony of seabird calls resounds from the cliff edge nesting sites and around the harbour estuary. The majestic fulmar skirts the cliff face, gliding gracefully on rigid wings over the coastal air currents. There are two large black birds along this coast; the white-faced

Nature Walk

Scrambling over slippery rocks and peering into limpid pools may reveal signs of life, such as:

SEA LEMONS — grazing marine organisms, these warty sea slugs produce long ribbons of eggs.

SEA URCHINS' SKELETONS or 'tests' are up to 8 inches (20 cm) across, and have white tubercles.

▼The vast stone cross near the top of Whitby's 199 steps is in memory of Caedmon, who was 'England's first poet'.

cormorant and the shag.

One of the few truly maritime plants seen along the coast is scurvygrass, which has a flat-topped cluster of white flowers. Its basal leaves are fleshy and a rounded, kidney shape. Scurvy is a disease caused by a deficiency of vitamin C, and was prevalent among seamen who ran short of fresh vegetables and fruit. The leaves of scurvygrass, which contain a good source of the vitamin, were often eaten by seafarers, hence the plant's name. The implication that the plant belongs to the grass family is false, though — it belongs to the cabbage family. Throughout the summer it provides a mass of white flowers along many parts of this coast.

Surrounded by moorland on three sides, Whitby has always had to seek its trade and communication with the world outside via the sea. The town's isolation from its hinterland did not begin to crumble until

▲ *Where the route crosses a small gully and stream, the path dips down through a mass of dense vegetation.*

the first stage-coach services to York in 1789, and gathered pace after 1836 when George Stephenson engineered a rail line to go over the moors to Pickering.

Whitby's religious and maritime history pervades the town. The gaunt ruins of the abbey ❶ dominate the headland scene, steadfast against the worst of unforgiving storms coming in off the sea. It was St Hilda who brought Christianity here in the 7th century. The famous Synod of Whitby was held in AD 664. The original abbey was destroyed by Danish invaders in the 9th century. The ruined abbey that you see today was built on the original site in 1078. Caedmon Cross ❶ commemorates a 7th-century farmworker turned monk, who had a vision in which he was called to sing a 'song of creation' which he

subsequently made famous.

On the opposite headland is the memorial to Whitby's greatest seaman, Captain James Cook. He stands near the much-photographed whalebone gateway, another famous East Coast landmark.

WILD BOAR

An 800-year-old crime is commemorated each year on the mud flats of Whitby harbour ❶. The details of the vicious attack upon the life of a peaceful monk came to light in an ancient manuscript written on vellum. In 1159, a monk from Whitby Abbey was living a life of solitude in a riverside refuge in the forest some 5 miles (8 km) upstream.

Three noblemen, who were out hunting, wounded a wild boar which ran into the hermit's chapel. He closed the door against the pur-

suing hounds. In their anger at such action, the hunters launched into the monk with their boar-staves. Before he died, the monk spared the lives of his murderers on condition of a penance, set in posterity upon the noblemen and their ancestors.

Thus it is that the time-honoured ritual of planting a 'Penny Hedge' of stakes on the mud flats above Whitby harbour takes place at 9 am on every eve of Ascension Day. The bailiff blows his ancient horn and cries 'Out on ye, Out on ye' (for this heinous crime). The name arises through the specification of 'a knife of a Penny Price', which was to be used in cutting the stakes of the hedge. Only once in recent times (1981) has the penance not been met and that was due to a freak tide that covered the mud flats to a depth of 8 feet (2.4 metres).

King of the Vampires

An ancient superstition held in parts of central and eastern Europe gave rise to the legend that the corpses of dead people could leave their graves at night and renew their lives by sucking the blood from people while they slept. Ghoulish tales born out of this superstition also suggested that the corpses could transform themselves into bats, cats, dogs, bears, wolves and other beasts. The innocent victims may themselves turn into vampires. These tales do have at least some basis in fact — a number of vampire bats in South America do sink their sharp teeth into other animals and lap their blood.

The author Bram Stoker used the vampire legend and his life-long interest in the supernatural to create the most famous of modern vampires — Count Dracula. His novel *Dracula*, published in 1897, was an instant success. He used Whitby as the setting for three spine-chilling chapters. In these, a Russian schooner crashes into Whitby pier in the teeth of a sudden gale; the captain is dead, the crew are missing and an 'immense dog' (the werewolf Dracula) slinks into the alleys below the cliff. Since the 1920s the now-famous story has been staged in plays and musicals.

The actual story has been filmed seven times, but the plot has also been twisted in every conceivable direction to make many sequels.

Actor Chistopher Lee is probably the most famous face of Count Dracula, having played the role in many horror films.

RICHMOND CASTLE

A medieval town, a forbidding castle and a ruined abbey

▲*Richmond Castle is one of England's earliest stone-built castles, dating back to 1071. The alderfly (inset) lives by water and is used as bait by anglers — it moves slowly, thus it is easily caught.*

The ruins of Richmond Castle **B** and Easby Abbey are linked by riverside paths through woods and meadows. Both castle and abbey have a peaceful history. Despite the castle's forbidding appearance, on a cliff above the river and commanding the entrance to Swaledale, it was never involved in war. It was founded in 1071 by Alan Rufus, one of William the Conqueror's followers.

HENRY VII

In the south-east corner is the two-storeyed Scollond's Hall, which was built at the same time and is probably the oldest hall in England. After 1485, the castle belonged to the Crown, when Henry Tudor, Earl of Richmond, became King Henry VII. The boundaries of the Market Place

A follow the line of the castle's outer bailey, from which medieval streets radiate. The walk starts here, then passes the church that houses the museum of the Green Howards.

The River Swale **C** begins at a height of over 2,000 feet (610 metres) on Birkdale Common as a moorland beck (brook). It is fed by numerous small streams in Upper Swaledale, maturing as it passes through Keld, Reeth and Richmond, before entering the Vale of York. It continues through rich agricultural land to join the River Ure, and eventually enters the Humber and the North Sea.

Easby Abbey **D** owes its existence to Roald, Constable of Richmond. He founded the monastery in 1151. The monks wore white habits and were known as the White Canons.

FACT FILE

- ✴ Richmond, 11 miles (18 km) south-west of Darlington

- Pathfinder 609 (NZ 10/SE 19), grid reference NZ 171009

miles 0	1	2	3	4	5	6	7	8	9	10 miles
kms 0 1 2 3 4 5	6	7	8	9 10 11 12 13 14 15 kms						

- ◗ Allow 2 hours, plus time to look around

- ▬ Good paths and tracks. Steep hills in Richmond

- P Large free car park in Victoria Road; disc parking at Market Square

- T United Bus Services

- Wide range of pubs, restaurants and cafés in Richmond

- WC By car parks and at Tourist Information Centre

- ⌐⌐ Richmond Castle, Easby Abbey

THE WALK

RICHMOND – ABBEY WOOD

This circular walk starts from the Market Place in Richmond.

1 From the top end of the Market Place **A**, walk past the church downhill to the bottom end. Turn right along Millgate. Follow this lane along, bearing left, then right below the castle **B**. Continue downhill to a small car park above the River Swale **C**. Half-way down the car park, follow the gravel path round to the left for a few paces, then take the steps on the right down to a small circular garden. Cross it, and take the steps at the far end down onto the riverside path. Turn left to follow the river bank along, soon going past a broad, grassy area.

2 Go underneath the stone bridge — the rough path and erosion make the going difficult here for a little way. After a short distance, the path bends away to the left. In about 50 yards (46 metres), take the broad track to the right, which goes through the woods above the river.

3 Where the path divides, take the footpath on the right, nearest the river. Keep to the path until it ends in a steep flight of stone steps on the left, topped by a stile. Cross it and turn right along the field edge to cross another stile. Walk past the house on the left and go through the gate onto the lane alongside Easby Abbey **D** and St Agatha's Church **E**. On leaving the abbey and church, you can make a short detour through the churchyard and up the lane to the left past the gatehouse; there is a good view here of the Abbey in its riverside meadow setting, with Richmond Castle in the distance. Return down the lane and bear to the left of the small car park. Go through a white-painted gate to rejoin the riverside path through woods.

4 After a short distance, turn right to cross the old railway bridge across the river. The route follows the track of the old railway line back to Richmond, crossed by a private drive several hundred paces further on. When you reach some steps on the right, follow them down to join another path nearer the river. Continue on in the same direction. Pass old station buildings and new swimming baths, then a small picnic area with tables, and cross the stile. Keeping away from the riverside, go ahead and uphill to another stile. Bear right to cross another stile into woods. Follow this path above the river, from where there are good views of the castle above the steep cliff on the other side. The path comes out into a playing field. At the far end, turn right to cross the old railway (now road) bridge over the river.

5 Continue straight on and go up the steep road ahead. Turn right up cobbled Cornforth Hill and go under the arch of the medieval gateway in the town walls **F**. Continue uphill along The Bar back to the Market Place.

As the endowments were increased, the monks were able to increase their numbers from 19 to 29. They led a tranquil existence in this quiet spot, although the peace was shattered by Scottish raids in the 14th century. Damage was also inflicted by English troops billeted here on their way to fight the Scots. A considerable amount of the ruins, however, remain today.

The parish church of St Agatha **E** stands next to the Abbey. It dates mainly from the 13th century, but the foundation of the church dates back further than the abbey itself. Near the altar is a replica of the Easby Cross, a piece of Anglo-Saxon sculpture dating back to the 7th or 8th century. The original was found in two pieces in 1932, and it is now in the Victoria and Albert Museum in London. The discovery of the cross suggests that there was once an Anglo-Saxon church or monastery on the site. Another unusual feature is the detailed 13th-century wall paintings, which have survived the centuries.

OLD RAILWAY LINE

The return route is over the old railway bridge and along the opposite river bank, following the line of the former railway. There are fine views of the abbey in its riverside setting. Further on, there are dramatic prospects of the castle, perched high on a cliff above the river. After recrossing the river back to the town, the way to the Market Place is up the steep Cornforth Hill and through a gate in one of the sections of the medieval town walls **F**.

◄ The monks at Easby Abbey belonged to the Premonstratensian Order, which was founded at Premontre in France.

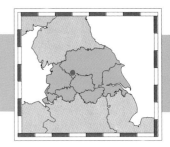

WHERE WOOL WAS KING

An historic market town and wool centre with an imposing castle

This is an all-weather walk on tarmac and a canal towpath, exploring the ancient wool town of Skipton. It begins by the library in the broad High Street. On most days, the street is lined with colourful market stalls. A plaque near Barclays Bank records the site of the market cross, pillory and stocks. The market is very old; its charter was granted in 1204. There were weekly markets for perishable goods, and larger fairs for leather, wine and salt. The chief trade, however, was in wool, which was the key to Skipton's success.

The first settlers arrived in the 7th century, when a group of Anglian sheep-farmers settled on the banks of the Eller Beck. In the *Domesday Book* of 1086, the town was called Sceapton, meaning sheep-town.

FACT FILE

✳ Skipton, 9 miles (14.4km) north-west of Keighley

🗺 Pathfinder 661 (SD 85/95), grid reference SD 990518

miles 0 1 2 3 4 5 6 7 8 9 10 miles
kms 0 1 2 3 4 5 6 7 8 9 10 11 12 13 14 15 kms

◗ Allow 1½ hours

▬ Pavements, lanes and canal towpath; suitable for all ages

P Large pay car park behind the High Street near start. Also at Cavendish Street, Coach Street and Spindle Shop Dam

T BR from Leeds. Several bus and coach companies

🍴 Pubs, restaurants and cafés in Skipton

WC Town centre car park

🏰 Skipton Castle: open daily, except Christmas Day. Craven Museum (free) in Town Hall opposite

▲*Springs Canal, a spur of the Leeds-Liverpool Canal, runs through Skipton. In the background is the chimney of Belle Vue Mill. The dunnock (inset) is a bird of both town and countryside.*

The town developed quickly as the need for labour in the wool industry — spinners (spinsters) and weavers (websters) — led to rapid population growth. The area behind the High Street, leading down from the castle, was filled in with housing around narrow yards. Some three-storey houses were built, with the top storey used as a weaving loft. Many of these yards survive, and have been attractively modernized. They are approached from the High Street by narrow alleyways, known as 'ginnels', which you pass as you walk down the High Street.

As the High Street merges with the cobblestones of Sheep Street, you pass a block of buildings which divides the main street. A plaque near the steps to the upper storey explains that this was the old Town Hall, and the cellars below were used as a lock-up for criminals.

CANAL BASIN

From Sheep Street, a right turn leads to the towpath by the Leeds–Liverpool Canal **Ⓐ**, whose basin has been developed as a marina.

Isaac Dewhurst built the 19th-century Belle Vue Mill **Ⓑ** on the

THE WALK

SKIPTON – STIRTON

The starting point of the walk is in Skipton's High Street, outside the library.

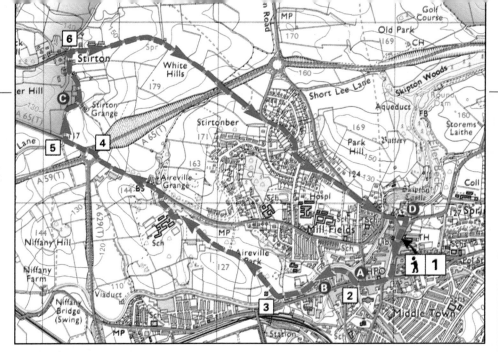

▶ **1** Walk south down the High Street, away from the castle. At the end of the road, bear right into Swadford Street. Walk on a little way, then cross the bridge over the Leeds-Liverpool Canal **A**.

▶ **2** Turn right onto the canal towpath and follow it round to the left, soon passing the tall chimney of Belle Vue Mill **B**, near the first swingbridge.

▶ **3** At the second swingbridge, cross the canal and go through the gates into Aireville Park.

Walk through the park, then cross the main road. Turn left and walk up to the roundabout.

▶ **4** Carry straight on at the roundabout, on the road to Kendal, then turn first right, into a lane signposted to Stirton.

▶ **5** Follow the lane, past the tithe barn **C** on your left, to the crossroads.

▶ **6** Turn right. This lane crosses the by-pass, and continues into Skipton. Just after Primrose Hill on the right, is the site of the Pinfold on the left. Soon afterwards you reach Mill Bridge, crossing the Eller Beck and Springs Canal. A little further on, turn left through the churchyard to reach the gatehouse of Skipton Castle **D**, near the starting point.

▲*Showing signs of its age, this tithe barn, on the outskirts of Stirton, has been somewhat roughly patched up.*

canal bank. Originally it produced worsted goods but switched to cotton when this overtook wool in importance. The mill kept pace with changing technology, and became renowned for 'Sylko' sewing threads. After World War II, Dewhursts was absorbed by English Sewing Ltd, but the mill was not closed until 1983. The Dewhurst family was very active in local affairs, giving Skipton its main recreation area, Aireville Park, through which the walk continues.

After a short walk along the Skipton to Kendal road, a quiet lane leads to the attractive village of Stirton. As you enter the village, you pass an old tithe barn **C** on your left. On a roadside verge there are the remains of double stocks.

The lane leading back towards Skipton is a drovers' road, a relic of the times when herds of Scottish cattle were driven to the southern markets. The hedgerows along this lane, full of interesting plants, are thought to be over 400 years old.

DOUBLE BRIDGE

Beyond the Pinfold, where stray horses and cattle were once impounded, you come to Mill Bridge, spanning both the Eller Beck and Springs Canal, a spur of the canal which was used to transport stone from a quarry. Next, you pass through the garden-like churchyard of the 12th-century parish church, emerging by the gatehouse of Skipton Castle **D**.

The strategic importance of Skipton was recognized by the Norman baron Robert de Romille, who sought to dominate the Aire Gap, a natural division between the north and south Pennines. He built the first castle on a rock above the Eller Beck gorge in the 11th century.

RESTORED CASTLE

The castle was added to in the 13th and 14th centuries. In the Civil War, it suffered badly from cannon damage and, when the Royalists were defeated, Cromwell ordered its destruction. However, the owner at the time, the remarkable and resolute Lady Anne Clifford, wrote to Cromwell, saying that if he 'pulled her castles about her ears' she would 'build them up again as fast'. She completely restored the castle and Holy Trinity Church next door.

In World War II, the castle had an unusual role, providing safe storage for many historic documents belonging to the British Museum.

▶*Skipton Castle, one of five castles restored by Lady Clifford. Her family motto 'Desormais' means 'Henceforth'.*

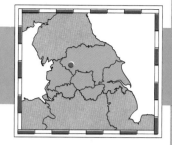

THE MARVELS OF MALHAM

8

NORTH YORKSHIRE

Through a limestone landscape to a dramatic dry waterfall

The village of Malham, in the Yorkshire Dales, is the gateway to an area of great scenic diversity. The underlying geology consists of water-soluble Great Scar limestone over a bed of impermeable Silurian slate. This has created a unique landscape of gorges and crags, pot-holes and pavements, lakes and waterfalls.

This circular walk begins in Malham Ⓐ itself. Despite its popularity with tourists, the village retains its charm. A clear stream runs through its centre, and on either side is a collection of attractive buildings that reflect the rich character of the area in their white limestone walls, mullioned windows, flag roofs and mellow, brown gritstone lintels and cornerstones.

Though Stone Age tools have

FACT FILE

- ✳ Malham, 9 miles (14.4km) north-west of Skipton

- 🗺 Outdoor Leisure Map 10, grid reference SD 900626

  miles 0 1 2 3 4 5 6 7 8 9 10 miles
  kms 0 1 2 3 4 5 6 7 8 9 10 11 12 13 14 15 kms

- ◔ Allow 4 hours

- ◣ Mostly on well-maintained footpaths, with some ascent and descent. Rough and muddy in places. One short, moderately difficult scramble in Gordale Scar; not suitable for the elderly or for young children

- 🅿 Car park at the start

- 🍺🍴 Several pubs, cafés and restaurants, and toilets in Malham

- Ⅰ National Park Visitors Centre open daily from Easter to October, otherwise weekends only, 9.30am-5pm

been discovered in nearby caves, the village itself dates from the 7th and 8th centuries, when the Angles established a wooden township here. In the Middle Ages, it was divided down the centre. The lands to the west of Malham Beck belonged to Fountains Abbey, while those to the east were part of the domain of Bolton Abbey.

▲ On the steep climb up to Gordale Scar, look back over the dramatic gorge with its sharp drop. Hart's tongue fern (inset) is found on limestone pavement; here it is growing with herb robert.

Behind the Old Smithy, a stone footbridge leads you out into the open countryside. The route goes through a network of small fields marked out by dry-stone walls. Many of them contain old stone barns whose lintels are carved with 18th- and 19th-century dates.

Near the limpid waters of Gordale Beck, the route passes through stands of oak and sycamore. From March to May, these resound to the distinctive drumming of green woodpeckers.

Soon you reach Janet's Foss Ⓑ, a

THE WALK

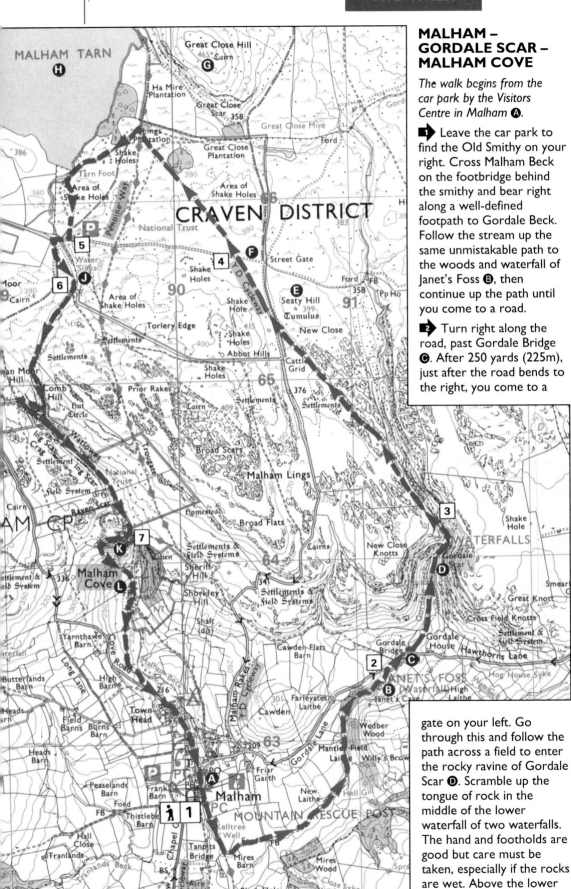

MALHAM – GORDALE SCAR – MALHAM COVE

The walk begins from the car park by the Visitors Centre in Malham **A**.

▶ Leave the car park to find the Old Smithy on your right. Cross Malham Beck on the footbridge behind the smithy and bear right along a well-defined footpath to Gordale Beck. Follow the stream up the same unmistakable path to the woods and waterfall of Janet's Foss **B**, then continue up the path until you come to a road.

▶ Turn right along the road, past Gordale Bridge **C**. After 250 yards (225m), just after the road bends to the right, you come to a

gate on your left. Go through this and follow the path across a field to enter the rocky ravine of Gordale Scar **D**. Scramble up the tongue of rock in the middle of the lower waterfall of two waterfalls. The hand and footholds are good but care must be taken, especially if the rocks are wet. Above the lower

fall, the path climbs some steep but easy steps to the top of the gorge.

▶ Above Gordale Scar, the path continues to rise gently before crossing open ground to reach a wooden stile over a stone wall. Seaty Hill **E** is above you to your right. Cross the stile and turn right along a surfaced road. In a short while, Mastiles Lane **F** crosses the route.

▶ The road bears left to follow Mastiles Lane, but you go straight ahead along an unsurfaced track, with Great Close **G** ahead and to your right. Follow a path swinging left across the field to follow the edge of a plantation. When you meet a beck issuing from Malham Tarn **H**, continue alongside it to a surfaced road.

▶ Turn right, go through a gate and over a low bridge. Take the signposted path immediately left to the Water Sinks **J**.

▶ Continue alongside a stone wall into a dry, rocky ravine. Leave at the other end by contouring right across an open hillside. Turn left at a signpost towards Malham Cove, crossing a stile over a wall to enter a long, dry valley. At its end, there is another wooden sign.

▶ Bear right to cross a limestone pavement **K**. Take care in wet weather, as the clints can be very slippery. After about 150 yards (135m), the pavement ends. Follow a signed path to the bottom of Malham Cove **L**. Continue along the path through the valley bottom, out of the cove onto a surfaced road. Bear left and walk down the road back to Malham village.

▲ *Follow the crystal-clear waters of Gordale Beck to the small, but spectacular, Janet's Foss waterfall.*

waterfall which, despite a relatively modest drop of 30 feet (9m), provides a fine spectacle. According to local legend, Janet is the queen of the fairies, said to live in a cave behind the wall, while Foss is a Viking word for waterfall; many place names in the area bear a Scandinavian influence. The pool below the fall was once used for dipping sheep. Workers would fortify themselves with strong ale before plunging into the cold waters.

PACKHORSE BRIDGE

The path briefly emerges on a surfaced road which bypasses Gordale Bridge ❸, a limestone arch over the beck. It was built for packhorses and is too narrow for vehicles. From here it is a short walk across open ground to the dramatic gorge of Gordale Scar ❹. Two waterfalls, one above the other, cascade into a cleft some

150 feet (45m) deep and just 30 feet (9m) wide at the base. The walls rise sheer, and even overhang in places.

The water issues from a hole in the rock. Today, there is a stream in the deep, narrow-sided valley above the Scar, but prior to 1730 there was a lake there. In that year, there was a great flood, which built up so much pressure on the damming rocks that it burst through them, sending the contents of the lake rushing through the ravine.

TONGUE OF TUFA

The lower fall has deposited a tongue of tufa, a light, airy limestone that precipitates out of lime-rich water as it tumbles through the air. You scramble up this to the base of the upper falls and climb a series of steps to the top.

The sun illuminates the gorge and the falls in the afternoon, though at any other time, and on grey days, it can be a relief to climb out onto the open moor above.

The path leads through jagged outcrops of gleaming white stone before joining a surfaced road beneath the flanks of Seaty Hill ❺. The summit of the hill is crowned by the grassy mound of a Bronze Age round barrow.

At Street Gate ahead, a crossroads slightly off the route, many old tracks intersect. The most important is Mastiles Lane ❻, which runs across Malham Moor from Ribblesdale to Kilnsey. The route is probably ancient, but today's lane dates from the 13th century, when

▼ *Above the meandering Gordale Beck rise sheer cliffs marking the entrance to Gordale Scar. On the open moor above it, the summit of Seaty Hill (right) is crowned by an ancient barrow.*

the monks of Fountains Abbey used it to drive cattle and sheep to and from their lands in the Lake District.

Later, the moors above Malham were the scene of great sheep and cattle fairs, where thousands of beasts from all over the North changed hands. Cattle drovers using the route would camp overnight in Great Close ❼. In the 18th century, the trade reached a peak, and as many as 5,000 head of cattle would graze the slopes beneath the crags of Great Close Hill on any one night.

Other animals were driven along Mastiles Lane. Teams of packhorses carried wool, and coal and calamine from nearby mines. Calamine, an ore of zinc used in the production of brass, was mined extensively in this area, particularly at the beginning of the 19th century.

The walk bears left around a walled plantation to the shores of Malham Tarn ❽. This beautiful lake owes its existence to an outcrop of a bed of Silurian slate that prevents the water from running away.

The wetlands on the western shore make up an important nature reserve, home to many different types of wildfowl. Nestling in the woods to the north is Malham Tarn House, a National Trust property

that is now a Field Studies Centre, providing much information concerning the area's wildlife.

The route follows the course of a stream issuing from the Tarn. This healthy, bubbling beck suddenly disappears into potholes in the limestone at the well-named Water Sinks ❾, and continues its course underground. The path continues into the dry valley of Watlowes, following a dry-stone wall along the former course of a stream long since gone underground. Steep cliffs pocked

with caves rise up on either side.

At the end of the dry valley is a limestone pavement **K**, formed by the action of rainwater on hairline vertical cracks in the exposed stone. Rain seeps into the cracks and gradually widens them. The blocks left between are known as clints and the deep fissures as grikes. While the bleached white clints, exposed to wind and weather, are hard as iron, the grikes form a stable, sheltered, micro-environment for several

▶ To the north of beautiful Malham Tarn lies the Field Studies Centre, now a National Trust property. Steep limestone cliffs at Malham Cove (below left) tower impressively above the rocky amphitheatre.

plants. Spleenworts thrive here, and the long, shiny leaves of hart's tongue fern are unmistakable.

From the pavement, there is an easy descent into the rock amphitheatre of Malham Cove **L**, which has inspired poems by both William Wordsworth and John Ruskin.

Massive faults in the limestone blocks have led to them falling away vertically, leaving cliffs some 300 feet (92m) high. The sheer, white walls are festooned with brightly-clad rock climbers for much of the year, while swifts make their nests in the rock-face cracks in summer.

The waterfall that was once here may well have resembled Niagara. Today, the water that fed it has found a new way down off the moors to leave it dry. The bright, clear stream that appears at the bottom of the cove, Malham Beck, does not come from Malham Tarn above, but from the disused mines of Pikedaw Hill, a little to the west.

From here, there is a gentle walk along the valley bottom and a road, past the distinctive architecture of Town Head Farm, back to Malham.

Droving Days

Before the advent of railways, livestock always moved from one place to another 'on the hoof'. Much of this traffic was local, with just a few animals being taken to market, but each year there were longer migrations. Hardy store cattle from Scotland and the North were taken to the lush pastures of East Anglia for fattening and slaughter, while Welsh animals went to Kent, Essex, and Buckinghamshire.

Larger herds were built up as animals were traded at various fairs along the way. They were taken along time-honoured routes that avoided, as far as possible, roads and towns. They spread out over open country, and met up again at passes or fords.

As they went, the drovers kept up a constant noise — shouting, blowing horns or playing bagpipes. This was partly to keep the cattle moving, and partly to warn farmers of their approach, so that they could pen their own beasts before they got caught up in the general movement.

The drovers' led nomadic lives. They usually slept under the stars with their charges, and would only occasionally stay or eat at an inn or farmhouse along the way. Consequently, they were often wild and unkempt in their appearance, but they were usually, of necessity, responsible men.

Much of the commerce in cattle was done on credit, and farmers had to rely on drovers to bring back the cash once the animals were sold. Drovers had to be licensed, or fall foul of the vagrancy laws. Only married men over 30 were taken on. They were entrusted not only with the cattle, but also with delivering letters and messages, and carrying out financial commissions. Several banks owed their origins to the financial arrangements made for drovers, and in Cromwellian times they were used as tax gatherers.

Drovers usually slept in the open with their sheep and cattle, but sometimes they stopped at an inn for refreshments.

A walk on the moors near a market town in the Dales

Wensleydale, which carves a bold path through the heart of the Yorkshire Dales, is characteristically broad and well wooded. During the Middle Ages it was known as Yoredale, after the River Yore, now Ure, which runs through it. The dale's current name comes from the small market town of Wensley at its eastern end.

This walk investigates the area on many levels, from the high tops and limestone scars of North Rakes Hill,

FACT FILE

- Hawes, 22 miles (35km) east of Kendal, on the A684

- Outdoor Leisure Map 30, grid reference SD 875898

miles 0 1 2 3 4 5 6 7 8 9 10 miles
kms 0 1 2 3 4 5 6 7 8 9 10 11 12 13 14 15 kms

- Allow 4 hours

- Reasonably easy going on paved paths, minor roads, moorland and field paths. Care needed near swallow holes and on river-banks. Walking boots are recommended, especially in the wet

- **P** Pay and display car park at start; may be full on market day (Tuesdays)

- Several pubs in Hawes and the Green Dragon Inn at Hardraw

- **¶** Cafés in Hawes and Hardraw

- **I** There is a small admission fee for the visit to Hardraw Force

◀*The graceful stone arches of Haylands Bridge cross the Ure at a site, just north of Hawes, where there was once a ford.*

▲*The outward route climbs towards the distinctive ridge of North Rakes Hill. Toothwort (right) is a parasite which grows from the roots of hazel.*

complete with sinister swallow holes, through wooded dales to the time-honoured wide, green field enclosures in the valley bottoms.

At the centre of the dale is the small market town of Hawes, which sprang up relatively recently, following the granting of its market charter by William III in 1700. Previously, it was a small farming village like many others in the area. Derived from 'Hals', meaning a pass between mountains, Hawes is a favourite stopping point for all who pass through.

The walk begins from the Upper Dales Folk Museum **A**, housed in the old station building; the railway is long gone. The hustle and bustle of the market town is soon left behind as the route winds along a part of the Pennine Way

THE WALK

HAWES – SEDBUSK – HARDRAW

The walk starts from the Upper Dales Folk Museum **A***, just to the east of the town centre in Hawes.*

1 Leave the car park via the access road, turn right, then immediately right again along Brunt Acres Road. About 50 yards (45m)

beyond a bridge over a disused railway line, turn left along a farm road, then immediately right along a paved route signposted 'Pennine Way'. At the end of the field path, go through a kissing-gate and continue in the same direction on the road. Cross the River Ure on Haylands Bridge **B**. After the road bears left, go

through a gated squeeze stile on your right, signposted 'Sedbusk 1¼ miles'. Follow the path over a footbridge and another squeeze stile to a road.

2 Cross and go over the stile opposite signposted 'Sedbusk ¼ mile'. Ignore the track directly ahead; instead bear half right towards a stepped stile on the far wall. Turn left up the road into Sedbusk **C**. Fork right through the village and

continue ahead along a farm track signposted 'North Rakes Hill'. Continue uphill to a farm gate.

3 Climb the ladder stile to your left just before the gate, and head uphill along a track. Follow the path to the right of a small clump of sycamore trees, then bear left behind them. Continue through a gate and head through another gate on your right. Keep ahead, following the contours of the hill round to a waymarker. Bear left along the obvious track over the open moor. Just beyond the next waymarker, take the left fork and head out over the tops.

4 Take a short detour to the cairn **D** on your left for a panoramic view. Return to the track and continue. Take the right fork and head to the right of a group of cairns in the distance. Cross Pike Slack, a small river, and continue, keeping close to the limestone outcrops on your right. Beware of the often deep swallow holes **E**, where moorland becks plunge into an underground cave system. Go to the right of the five cairns, and follow the path over moorland. Cross Shivery Gill with care. At a footpath junction, bear left. Turn left along the road. Just beyond a cattle grid you may wish to pause to admire the view from Sowry Head **F**.

5 After another 300 yards (270m), turn right on a footpath signposted 'High Shaw'. Follow the path to the right of a barn, over a ladder stile and down the hill, keeping close to the dry-stone wall on your left. At the bottom, climb over the ladder stile and walk along the river-bank, taking

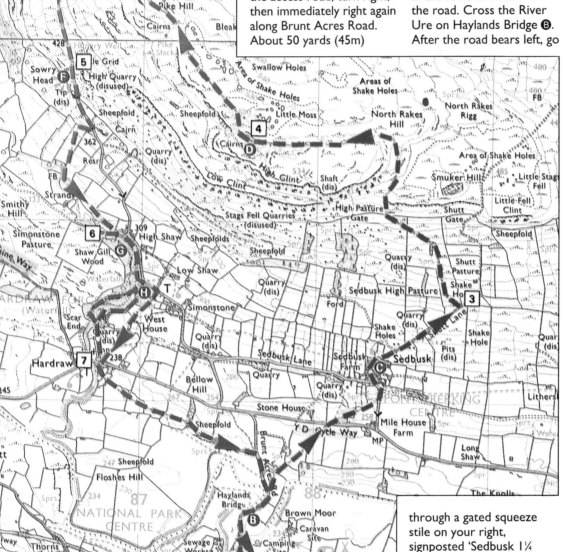

Nature Walk

THE CURLEW has a long, curved beak, a white V on its back and a heavily barred whitish underwing. Its wingbeats are slow and steady.

THE EGGS are pointed in shape, and a grassy, greenish colour, spotted with brown. Clutches of four are laid between April and May in a hollow.

long-distance footpath.

Before Haylands Bridge **B** was constructed in 1820, wheeled vehicles had to ford the Ure here. Now, the area is used for recreation, with fishing in the river, a cricket pitch on one side and a small nine-hole golf course on the other.

Throughout April and May, the low-lying meadows around the Ure resound to the bleating of newborn lambs, which chase around the fields madly and may even approach and investigate your boots. Although there are plenty of sheep around Hawes, milk is its main product, and has been since the railway came in 1878. Every night, a train full of milk left Hawes for London, and even now over 6,000 gallons (27kl) a day make the journey by road to the capital.

LEAD MINING

Beyond Sedbusk **C**, the route heads up North Rakes Hill past some limekilns, evidence of an industry that thrived here over 100 years ago, along with lead mining. Fortunately for the dale, demand fell and the local economy returned to the more pastoral employment of farming.

The wild moorland on North Rakes Hill is the preserve of the curlew, whose wailing cry epitomizes the atmosphere of these high tops. The males announce their readiness to take a mate and own a territory by gliding from the clear skies on outstretched wings, their strongly downcurved bills making them unmistakable.

From the cairns **D** on High Clint there is a spectacular view if the weather is kind. Ahead are the flat-topped heights of Ingleborough and the steep slope of Pen-y-Ghent. Down below, the tiny houses of Hawes nestle on the banks of the impressive Ure; from this remote vantage point the villages along its course appear totally insignificant.

Behind you are the rambling moors of Abbotside Common, where a multitude of becks and springs bisects the peaty soil and keeps the sphagnum beds moist. Care must be taken here, as numerous swallow holes **E** have formed in the limestone bedrock. At these points, foaming moorland becks plunge deep underground and dance around the cave systems. Any apertures without a disappearing

▲ *A typical view of the Dales landscape as you approach Shivery Gill, with small fields, dry-stone walls and hills.*

stream are known as shake holes; the waters that created them have been commandeered by new swallow holes further upstream.

While carefully crossing the narrow, fast-flowing beck, appropriately named Shivery Gill, glance upstream to see a small, attractive waterfall that tumbles furiously from the fells through a narrow limestone ravine. Beginning near the summit of Lovely Seat, the waters endure a punishing journey from Sod Hole Gill to the relatively

great care at one point where erosion has narrowed the path. Cross another ladder stile and continue for about 30 yards (27m). Cross the stile on your left into a field. Follow the path through fields to some buildings. Take the path to the right of the farm gate to a road. Turn right.

6 After 60 yards (55m), at the bottom of the first incline, go down steps on your left and continue left along a paved path by a river-bank **G**. Beyond a gate, bear left to join a minor road. Turn right along the main road. After 100 yards (90m) climb the ladder stile on your right. Walk downhill along a farm track. At the farm buildings, turn right through a squeeze stile. Follow the path, through a series of stiles and gates, to a road and turn right to the Green Dragon Inn.

7 (To visit Hardraw Force **H**, go through the pub. Follow the path to the falls, then return through the pub.) Cross the road. Follow a footpath to the right of the café, bearing left after 50 yards (45m). Follow the paved path through fields over a series of gated squeeze stiles. At a road, turn right to return to Hawes and the start.

tranquil reaches of the Ure.

On the road heading south to Hawes, pause at the signposted viewpoint of Sowry Head **F** and look across to the Hearne Coal Road, which runs north-west beyond Fossdale Farm. At the beginning of the century, villagers made regular trips along this route by horse and cart to purchase coal from small mines close to the top of Great Shunner Fell on your far right. The coal cost 2s 8d (13p) for 8 hundredweight (406kg), but the

▲*In contrast with the higher becks, the River Ure is a broad river, sweeping through farmland and woodland.*

buyers often wasted a full day making the journey there and back. One enterprising man started a coal delivery round, and simply doubled the price of the coal to cover the cost of his services.

Quite soon, the route leaves the road and passes through fields before dropping via a wooden stair, which needs to be descended with care, to a magical wooded river-bank **G**. The path is paved, but this does not detract from the feeling of undisturbed natural beauty that fills the valley.

In June, the scent of wild garlic mingles with the sweet smell of honeysuckle to provide a perfect aromatic accompaniment for the Upper Hardraw Falls, which cascade over great slabs of rock. Primroses punctuate the green carpet

▶ *The Upper Hardraw Falls are in a delightful wooded valley that is full of flowers and birdsong in spring.*

and toothwort, one of few plants that are parasitic, grows in the rocky crevices. Pied flycatchers nest in the tree holes, dippers walk under the mini rapids and woodpeckers hammer noisily in the canopy.

BRASS BANDS

After paying a small fee and passing through the Green Dragon Inn, it is a short walk to the majestic Hardraw Force **H** (see box), which highlights perfectly the power of the dale. In Victorian times, the acoustic qualities of the enclosed ravine were recognized and regular brass band competitions were held. These now occur each September and provide an

added attraction for the tiny hamlet of Hardraw. To listen to the melodic strains of a brass band is an ideal way to end a tiring day on the high fells and to prepare for the walk along an easy section of the Pennine Way back into the town of Hawes.

Hardraw Force

After many practice runs over small falls in the woods above, Fossdale Beck plummets 96 feet (29.3m) into the depths of Hardraw Scar to become England's highest unbroken waterfall above ground. Since Victorian times, the spectacle, painted by Turner, has attracted crowds of tourists.

The waters have worn away the soft shale behind the fall, allowing those who dare to walk behind the fall and stare out through the curtain of water. Legend tells of a sheepdog that explored a cave behind the fall, disappeared for a while, then surfaced from the underground

system at Cotterdale totally hairless.

It is entirely due to a previous landowner, Lord Wharncliffe, that we can enjoy the falls today. After a horrendous flood washed away bridges and damaged several villages towards the end of the 19th century, the overhanging lip of the Force was destroyed, leaving the water to spill unceremoniously down the shale cliff of the scar. Realizing what a loss this was, he commissioned workers to rebuild the lip and so restore Hardraw Force to its former glory.

The waters of Hardraw Force spill over a wooded cliff in a solid plume.

NORTH YORKSHIRE

◄Cattle grazing in stone-walled fields above Osmotherley. The gorse and bracken at the field edges and on the moors are much loved by the whinchat (inset), a summer visitor to Britain.

A country walk round a nonconformist village and a Catholic chapel

This walk, at the edge of the North York Moors National Park, gives a flavour of the varied natural habitats of the region: conifer plantations and mixed woodland; fields and open moorland, a reservoir and a clear stream. At its heart is the picturesque village of Osmotherley, and its legacy of religious and secular buildings.

North of the village, where the walk begins, is Cod Beck Reservoir **Ⓐ**. It was created for the Yorkshire Water Board in 1953. A stone quarry was submerged, along with a group of cottages at Wild Goose Nest, where there was once an illicit still.

LONG-DISTANCE PATH

You head across open moor onto an old, straight track through a conifer plantation. Green Lane, bordered by honeysuckle, rowan, dog roses, hawthorn and gorse, descends gently out of the trees. There are good views of Osmotherley to your right.

The route turns off to follow the Cleveland Way. This, Britain's second oldest long-distance path, is

a well waymarked route that runs 93 miles (150km) around the Moors from Helmsley to Filey Brigg.

You cross Cod Beck and continue through woodland to Osmotherley. The village has connections with John Wesley, first invited here in 1745 by Peter Adams, a former Franciscan friar. The Methodist chapel **Ⓑ** in Chapel Passage, built in 1754, is one of the earliest nonconformist chapels in England and is

still in use today. Wesley often preached there, standing on a stool to make up for his short stature. The stool can still be seen in the chapel.

MARKET CROSS

The market cross **Ⓒ** was erected in 1874 to replace an ancient one, the top of which can be seen outside No. 12 West End. A Saturday market was held here until 1823. The stone table, used as a stall for butter and fish, was pressed into service as an impromptu pulpit when Wesley preached at open air services here.

The Church of St Peter **Ⓓ** stands on the site of a pre-Norman building, stones from which can be seen in the porch. The fine font and doorway are Norman, and date from around 1190, but much of the church was destroyed by Scottish raiders in 1322 and restored in 1350. An interesting feature is part of an ancient hog-back tombstone, both of its ends supported by a carved bear.

▼*The market cross and the stone table from which John Wesley once preached.*

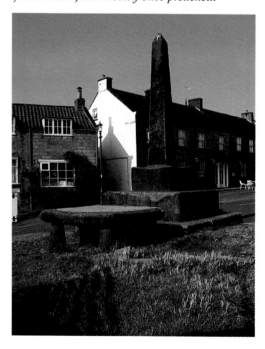

FACT FILE

※ Osmotherley, 6 miles (9.6km) east of Northallerton, off the A19

🗺 Outdoor Leisure Map 26, grid reference SE 468992

miles 0 1 2 3 4 5 6 7 8 9 10 miles
kms 0 1 2 3 4 5 6 7 8 9 10 11 12 13 14 15 kms

🕐 Allow 3 hours

🥾 Undulating walk, with gentle climbs. Paths can be very wet after rain

🅿 Two small car parks at start

🍴 Three pubs and a café in Osmotherley

🚻 Near the market place in Osmotherley

THE WALK

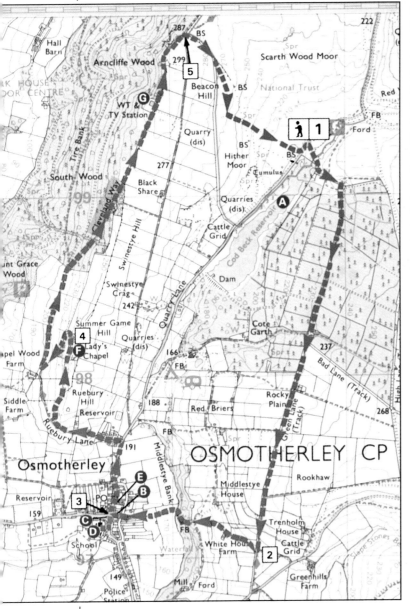

COD BECK RESERVOIR— OSMOTHERLEY

The walk starts at a small car park at the north end of Cod Beck Reservoir Ⓐ, opposite a standing stone marked 'Lyke Wake Walk'.

1 Follow a small path down to the stream and cross the stepping stones (after heavy rain, walk along the road away from the reservoir, cross the footbridge, then return on the other bank of the stream). Continue uphill, with a plantation to your right. Climb a ladder stile into the plantation and follow the main track ahead between the trees. When the plantation ends, continue ahead on the same track for nearly ¾ mile (1.2km) to a sign for the Cleveland Way.

2 Pass through a squeeze stile to your right to join the Cleveland Way. Follow this broad track gently downhill, passing to the right of a house and crossing stiles. At the bottom of the hill, cross a footbridge waymarked with an acorn. Continue on the Way, uphill through trees and across fields to a lane. Cross this and pass

between two cottages, with a Methodist chapel Ⓑ on your right. Go under an archway to the main street. The market cross Ⓒ is across the road.

3 Turn left along the street, then right along School Lane to the church Ⓓ. Return to the main street and turn left. Continue ahead past the Old Hall Ⓔ. At the end of the village, turn left down Ruebury Lane on the Cleveland Way. Shortly after passing the last house on your right, turn right on a path signposted to the Lady's Chapel. Where the track ahead is marked 'Private', go left up some steps to the chapel Ⓕ.

4 Go past the chapel and follow a path downhill alongside a wall to your left, to the Cleveland Way. Turn right. Follow the Way ahead into a wood. Bear right at the fork a little way into the trees. Continue ahead past the BT station Ⓖ.

5 About 200 yards (180m) beyond a trig point, go through a gate and across a stile. Turn right and follow a peaty path downhill though the heather back to the start.

▼*Bordered by conifers, Cod Beck Reservoir is a lovely stretch of water.*

The Old Hall Ⓔ in North End was bought by Lady Juliana Walmsley in 1665 for the use of Franciscan friars. They were forced to leave in 1832, but returned in 1969. The top floor is now a lovely Catholic church, entered through the garden.

The friars served pilgrims visiting the Chapel of Our Lady of Mount Grace Ⓕ, which stands on a hilltop outside the village. It was built by Carthusian monks from Mount Grace Priory early in the 16th century, on the site of an earlier shrine, and rebuilt in 1960.

The large, well-preserved ruins of the priory, which was founded in 1398, are at the bottom of the hill to the west of the route.

As you head north once again on the Cleveland Way, you pass a BT microwave radio station Ⓖ, 982 feet (299m) above sea level, which receives and transmits television and telecommunications signals.

The last stretch of the walk crosses open moorland. Red grouse, wheatears and curlews may be spotted here, while adders and common lizards, though not often seen, live among the heather, bilberry and bracken. Hares are a common sight as you return across the open hillside to the start.

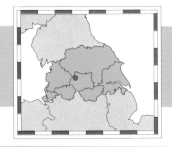
A beautiful walk around the country that inspired *Wuthering Heights*

This walk explores some of the most evocative landscape of the Yorkshire Pennines. The desolate moors, which so inspired the Brontë sisters, rise majestically above the steep-sided valleys — a vast expanse of treeless moorland, crag and heather through which narrow streams and cloughs (gorges) twist their way, forming little valleys of delicate beauty.

Drystone walls criss-cross the hillsides in elaborate patterns, punctuated by barns and remote farmhouses, many of them dating from the 17th century, and some clustered in hamlets and villages that have changed little over the centuries. This upland landscape contrasts, often starkly, with the bustling Victorian mill towns and

FACT FILE

✳	Haworth, West Yorkshire
▭	Pathfinder 682 (SE 03/13) and Outdoor Leisure Map 21, grid reference SE 029372

miles 0   1   2   3   4   5   6   7   8   9   10 miles
kms 0   1   2   3   4   5   6   7   8   9   10   11   12   13   14   15 kms

◔	5 hours
▰	Paths can be muddy and overgrown. Sturdy footwear (preferably walking boots) strongly recommended
P	Haworth Parsonage car park, at top of village. There are alternative car parks in the village at busy times
T	Park-and-ride steam train service from Keighley, or Ingrow to Haworth Station at weekends and holiday times, avoid congestion
WC	In Haworth and Oakworth
⊞ ⊤	Wide choice of refreshments in Haworth. Pubs in Stanbury and Oakworth

industry in the larger valleys, including Haworth itself, still served by a restored steam railway.

The old part of Haworth **Ⓐ** has a steep, cobbled Main Street, leading down from the church, with alleys and courts branching off it, but the village expanded in Victorian times, stretching down the hillside towards the river and railway.

DARK SATANIC MILLS

At the time of the Brontës this was a thriving and squalid early industrial town. It was towns like Haworth that provided the backbone of Victorian industrial wealth. Many of the older cottages still retain their weaving lofts, with their multi-paned windows to provide the weavers with maximum light. These lofts pre-dated the new water and steam-powered mills.

Haworth had grown rapidly at the beginning of the 19th century and was overcrowded and without any sanitation or proper drainage.

▲ *The wild bleakness of Haworth Moor and the ruins of Top Withens were the inspiration for* **Wuthering Heights.** *(inset) Wild moorland harebells.*
▼ *The steep Main Street of Haworth.*

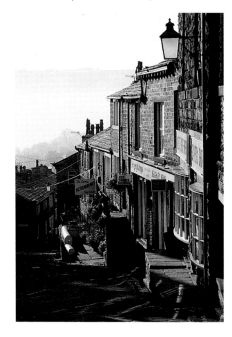

THE WALK

HAWORTH – STANBURY – OAKWORTH

The walk begins at the Brontë Parsonage Museum in Haworth **A**.

1 Walk down the hill towards the church **B**; turn right through a kissing gate below the churchyard, along an enclosed stone-paved way.

2 At the footpath junction turn right, signposted Brontë Falls, up to the road. Sowden's Farm **D** is across fields on the left. Cross the road and enter the Penistone Hill Country Park. Take the narrow footpath bearing left across the moor ahead and Penistone Hill **E**. Continue over the brow of the hill.

3 Keep left around the edge of the old quarry and follow the clear track round to the right, before eventually bearing left down to the road.

4 Walk a few yards down the road and then take the track on the right to Drop Farm. Continue straight ahead with the wall on your left to a footpath junction. Follow the line of yellow posts across the moorland.

5 At the track turn left. Just before the farm take the footpath on the right, cross

over the bridge and walk down a shallow ravine to Brontë Falls **F**.

6 Cross the stream at the stone bridge — Brontë Bridge — and head directly up the hill. Go through the gate and turn right towards Stanbury. Follow the footpath to a track and turn right into the village of Stanbury **G**.

7 Walk to the far end of the village and take the green lane on the left that runs behind the village. Continue for about 150 yards (135 metres) and then go through a gate on the right, following a field path down to a stream. Cross the

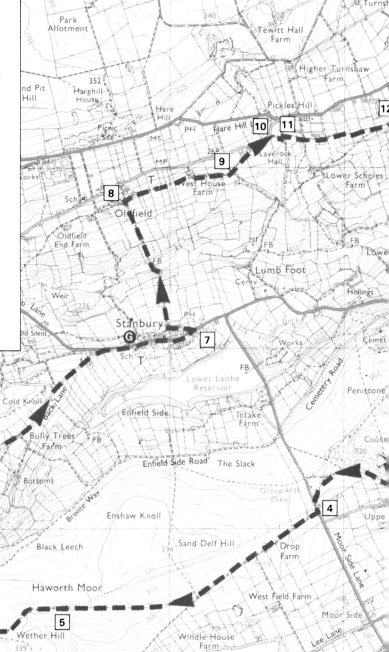

The Parsonage at Haworth was home to the remarkable Brontë family and now houses Brontë memorabilia.

Also, refuse was simply left to rot in the streets. Not surprisingly, disease, particularly typhoid, was rife. Even in the 1850s half the children died before they were six and the average life expectancy was 25 years old — figures that equalled the worst London slums.

This high mortality rate led to overcrowding in the graveyard, until finally the old Parish Church,

with its cottage windows, had to be pulled down in 1879 because of the excessive number of bodies in its vaults and in the nearby graveyard. It was threatening the very health of the town. And it is quite sobering to realize that the Parsonage obtained all its drinking water from a well sunk into the ground of that cemetery. The present church **B**, built in 1880, has a chapel in memory of the Brontë family.

Behind the church is the Black Bull Inn **C** where Branwell Brontë spent much of his time. He drank

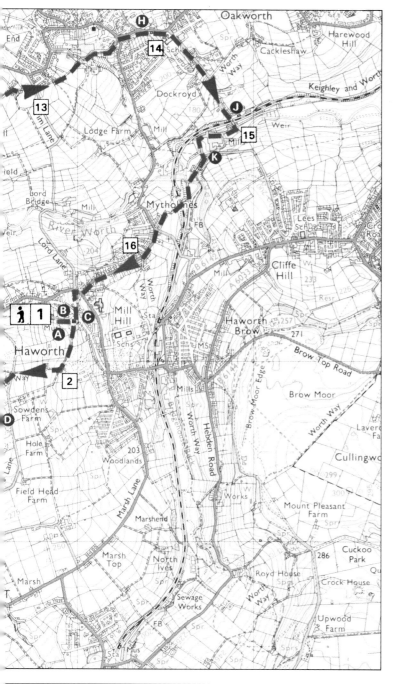

bridge and continue uphill to another gate, pass through a third gate and go up the field to a farm track. Turn right on to the path leading to Manor House Farm at Oldfield.

8 Continue straight ahead through two small gates, through a farm, following a field path to West House Farm. Look for a small stile in the wall. Cross the stile to pass the farm house on the left. Bear right and then go straight ahead to a small gap in the wall. Follow the field path until arriving at a track.

9 Continue straight ahead with a barn on the right, through a gate to a second track. Walk up the embankment to go through a gap in the wall opposite and follow the field path past a new house to take the gate on the left to the road.

10 Turn right and as the road bends and goes uphill, walk through the small gap in the wall on the right and follow the field path to a farm. Go through a gate, turn right and cross the farmyard to another gate opposite a barn.

11 Cross two fields and continue straight ahead along a walled track between a row of cottages. As the track bends to the

right cross the stone stile to the left of the house. Follow the stone stiles across the fields until reaching a farm track.

12 Turn left up the hill to a stile and continue across fields to a farm. Turn left, following the track right round the farm to a gate. Follow the field path to another farm and then turn right down a track to the road.

13 Cross the road and go over a small stone stile on the right. Continue along the footpath, crossing a track down to an old mill. Here, the path may become overgrown with nettles during the summer. Turn right and continue to road junction. Follow the Colne Road downhill past Holden Park **H**.

14 Continue to the bottom of the hill. Turn right down Station Road to arrive at Oakworth Railway Station **J**.

15 Walk along the road past Vale Mill **K** and over the bridge. Reach Valefold Cottages and take the footpath to Mytholmes Lane.

16 At the road continue uphill into Haworth and to the Parsonage at the start of the walk.

himself to an early grave with a mixture of Yorkshire ale and opium.

FIRE AND BRIMSTONE

Just outside Haworth is a 17th-century farmhouse **D** that became the setting for 18th-century revivalist meetings led by the English Evangelical preacher William Grimshaw. Grimshaw was a close friend of John Wesley and his fiery zeal attracted congregations from miles around, with meetings often continuing until five o'clock in the morning. Grimshaw would often

leave during the Psalm to bring in idlers off the street and from public houses to hear his sermon.

Penistone Hill **E** appears in *Wuthering Heights* as Penistone Crags, a local beauty spot near Thrushcross Grange. The quarry here provided the stone for the paving blocks in the high street, and for the dark buildings of Haworth. Looking at the now disused gritstone quarries on the edge

'Owd Timmy', the last handloom weaver, enjoying a pipe at his cottage.

of the moor it is hard to imagine that as late as the 1920s a hundred men hewed stone here. Penistone Hill is now a 180 acre (73 hectare) Country Park and from the summit there is a spectacular view across the bleak, open Pennines.

WUTHERING HEIGHTS

Brontë Falls **F**, which tumble into Salden Beck, was a favourite spot with the Brontë sisters and is described in their poems and letters. A few yards down the stream is the Brontë seat which is hewn out of a single piece of rock. And high up on the Moors is Top Withens, the ruin of a lonely farmhouse which is said to have been the inspiration for Emily Brontë's well-loved novel *Wuthering Heights*.

The Four Brontës

Charlotte, Emily, Anne and their brother Branwell developed an intense creative partnership which was to lead to the writing of some of the greatest novels of 19th-century English fiction, including Charlotte's *Jane Eyre* and *Villette*, Emily's *Wuthering Heights* and Anne's *The Tenant of Wildfell Hall*. Only Branwell failed to fulfil his early promise and died of a broken heart, opium and drink.

The Brontë Falls (top) were a favourite haunt of the sisters and much of their poetry is deeply descriptive of the moods of the countryside surrounding Haworth. The Brontë seat (above) may well have witnessed the first few words of a novel.

Stanbury **G** is a typical Pennine moorland village. It was the home of Timothy Feather, known as 'Owd Timmy', the last handloom weaver in Yorkshire. The steam-powered West Riding mills of the 19th century saw the demise of this old cottage industry, but 'Owd Timmy' pursued his craft until his death in 1910 aged 85. His loom is on display in Cliffe Castle Museum in nearby Keighley.

Holden Park **H** was once the home of Sir Isaac Holden, but is now a delightful and unusual garden laid out in his memory by his grandson, Francis Illingworth. Surrounding the bowling green are elaborate stone grottos and walkways that are a delight to explore.

THE DAYS OF STEAM

Oakworth Station **J**, which is on the Keighley and Worth Valley line has been beautifully restored as a Victorian country halt, albeit with a 1950s flavour. Old advertisements, a genteel ladies' waiting room, a ticket machine and gaslights all add to the atmosphere. On the platform stand milk churns and old-fashioned leather luggage still waiting to be collected, and the staff are dressed in immaculate period costume. This was the station used for the film *The Railway Children*.

The 4½ mile (7.2 km) Keighley and Worth Valley Railway is one of the finest restored steam railways in the country and runs regular daily steam services in the summer, and

at weekends during the winter months. The railway was originally opened in 1867, not only to carry passengers but also to bring raw materials to the valley's mills, like Vale Mill which lies close to Oakworth Station.

Vale Mill **K** dates from the 1780s and, as in many other Yorkshire mills, cotton was originally spun here. During the 19th century the mill eventually turned to worsted manufacturing and developed into the present elaborate complex.

Vale Mill was once owned by a strict Methodist family, the Sugdens, and the employees were forbidden to drink or to gamble, and those courting couples that 'got into trouble' either had to marry or face losing their jobs.

The walk can be shortened by catching a train at Oakworth Station back to Haworth.

The beautifully restored station at Oakworth is a perfect period piece.

SUMMER WINE COUNTRY

A walk through a deep Pennine valley

The Pennine town of Holmfirth could not be more typical of the West Yorkshire scene, with its stone walls, steep streets and moorland setting. Its distinctive character made it an ideal choice for the location of many of the episodes in the television series, *Last of the Summer Wine*, first shown in 1972. The walk includes visits to a number of places seen regularly in the series.

COTTAGE INDUSTRY

The buildings in Holmfirth are made and roofed with local stone, and some still retain weaver's windows on the upper storey that allowed more light to reach the hand looms. There are several split-level, four-storey houses set on hillsides, with a two-storey section on the lower level and another above, reached from the upper level. In the wooded valleys around the

FACT FILE

✳ Holmfirth, 6½ miles (10 km) south of Huddersfield on the A6024 and A635

▱ Pathfinder 714 (SE 00/10), grid reference SE 143083

miles 0   1   2   3   4   5   6   7   8   9
kms 0   1 2 3 4 5 6 7 8 9 10 11 12 13 14 15

◕ Allow 4 hours

▲ Walking shoes or boots are recommended

P A large car park behind the Postcard Inn, Huddersfield Road, Holmfirth

T Bus to and from Huddersfield, Leeds and Marsden

🍴 Inns and cafés in Holmfirth

WC Holmfirth, near post office

⌂ Holmfirth Postcard Museum open Mon–Sat, 10am–4pm, Sun 12–4pm

▲ *Looking south-east from the New Mill Dike you can see a waterfall just inside the oak wood. Black-faced sheep (inset) graze on the coarse grass of the Yorkshire Moors.*

town are mills which were once powered by water from the streams.

In Holmfirth itself, a walk up Cooper Lane ➊ gives a good view back over the rooftops. To the left of the church tower, you will see a terrace of three houses with pointed lintels. This was used as Clegg's home in the television series, with Pearl and Howard living at the other end of the lane. At the foot of Cooper Lane, in a basement, is the *Last of the Summer Wine* exhibition. This includes some of the gadgets used by Seymour and photographs from the filming of the series.

At the Postcard Museum ➋ is a display of postcards selected from a collection of over 30,000 cards. Admission costs £1.00 for adults and 50p for children. A video presentation shows some films from the early days of the cinema, and

THE WALK

HOLMFIRTH

The walk begins at the car park in Holmfirth.

1 From the car park, walk up to Huddersfield Road and turn left. Walk along the road to the end of Cooper Lane **A**, on your right. Continue past the traffic lights to the Holmfirth Postcard Museum **B**. Then walk on to the Toll House Bookshop **C**, on your left.

2 Turn left to Upper Bridge in Hollowgate **D**. Follow Hollowgate to the left; this leads into Victoria Square and the church in Towngate. Turn right just before the church into the paved courtyard. Sid's café **E** is on your right. Climb the steps beside the church on your left, turn left, then fork right to some steps that lead into Bunkers Hill. At the road junction, turn back right to the next road junction.

3 Turn left and walk up the steep road, and take the first road, hard back left, before Rose Cottage. Pass below Moor View Cottage and continue climbing up the twisting road to a T-junction at the top of New Laithe Lane. Turn left, then immediately right along a grassy track for 150 yards (137 metres).

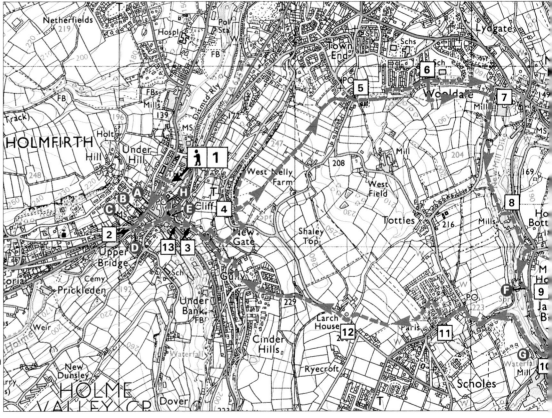

4 The route now turns right through a gateway, but you should first walk along the lane for 200 yards (183 metres) to see the extensive views over Holmfirth and the surrounding hills before returning to the gateway. Keeping the stone wall on your right, turn right, then left into a farm lane between stone walls. Carry straight on past the farm and fork right between stone walls down to a lane. Turn left down to the road.

5 Turn right, then first left down a stone lane. About 10 yards (9 metres) down the lane, turn left past a green gate, to go along a signposted footpath. A further 10 yards (9 metres) beyond the sign, turn left down a shrubby path that leads to a track.

Turn left down the track that descends to a housing estate, then turn right through the estate.

6 Here you have an option. You can continue on the pavement to a road junction and turn right into Green Hill Bank Road; or you can turn right into the playing field, and turn left behind the houses. At the end of the field, a path beside a wooden fence

there is a Victorian post-box that can be used to mail the reproduction cards on sale, all of which receive a special collector's stamp.

A section of the museum is also devoted to the 1852 Holmfirth Flood Disaster, when the Bilberry Dam burst. The dam, which stood some 3½ miles (5.6 km) further up the valley, had been constructed 15 years earlier. After heavy rain on 4th

◀ *The hills east of Holmfirth provide extensive views over the setting for the TV series* **Last of the Summer Wine**.

leads down to steps into Green Hill Bank Road, where you turn right.

7 Walk up the road. At the top of the hill, opposite Number 47, take the left fork down a stone-walled lane. At the bend, carry straight ahead through a squeeze stile beside the gate, and follow the path along the hillside. There are views down to a waterfall. Pass into an oak wood, then follow the path which leads to a mill. Turn left, then right past the buildings.

8 Cross over the stream at the mill entrance, then turn right in front of the houses along a track beside the stream. When the track forks left past a ruined house, continue straight ahead on a path above the stream, that leads to a newly restored mill. Take the steps **F**, to the left of the main building that lead up to a road.

9 Turn right and in 200 yards (183 metres), fork right along the road into Jackson Bridge.

10 Turn right to the White Horse Inn **G**. Walk along Scholes Road, following the wooded valley on your right. After 1/2 mile (800 metres), turn left into Paris Road.

11 Turn right up Cherry Tree Walk. Take the second turning left into a cul-de-sac and turn right along a signposted path. Pass through a stone squeeze stile and cross the field to a stile in the field corner. Follow the wall on your left, passing the quaintly named hamlet of Paris on the left. Cross two more stiles, then cross a stile between two gates. Cross three more stiles over the fields that lead into a lane. Turn left to the road.

12 Turn right along the footpath beside the road. At the fork, bear left and descend along the road back into the town of Holmfirth.

13 Just before you reach the main road, turn right and take the steps leading into the square where Sid's café is situated. Turn left, then right into Towngate and walk to the stone pillar **H**, set above the car park. Pass the toilets and turn left past the post office. At the end of the street, turn right along the white-railed path. Cross the second footbridge to return to the car park.

▲ *The café in the courtyard off Towngate will be familiar to fans as Sid and Ivy's.*

▼ *This pretty little waterfall is a short way upstream from the mill.*

metres) above sea level, before descending to Woodhead. Acts to establish turnpike roads could be obtained from Parliament by trustees who could then charge tolls and improve the roads. Toll-paying was taken so seriously that anyone found guilty of damaging or pulling down a toll gate could be transported for seven years.

When you reach the Upper

February, the dam was full and when the retaining wall collapsed at about 1 o'clock the following morning, 86 million gallons (390 million litres) of water swept down onto the town, carrying with it bales of wool, masonry, uprooted trees and even steam boilers.

LOSS OF LIFE

That night 81 inhabitants of the valley lost their lives, and 7 bridges, 24 industrial buildings, 27 cottages and 7 shops were totally destroyed. Because of Holmfirth's geographical location — it lies in a steep-sided valley surrounded by high moors — it has always been at risk from flood, and serious floods also occurred here in 1771, 1821 and 1944.

The Toll House Bookshop **C** stands on the site of the former toll house. The original building was washed away in the 1852 flood, drowning the occupants, Samuel Greenwood and his wife and child. The toll house was used to collect tolls on the Enterclough Bridge to Woodhead turnpike road. The road climbs to a height of 1,718 feet (524 Bridge **D**, look upstream to see the row of houses on the right that were used as the home of *Last of the Summer Wine*'s Nora Batty and Compo, who lived in the basement of the house. On the left of the bridge is the Elephant and Castle, a former coaching inn standing beside the turnpike road. On the side of the second door is a brass plate indicating the height reached by floodwater after a cloudburst on Whit Monday, 29th May 1944.

Standing on the paved churchyard of Holy Trinity Church, Sid's

Comic Cards

Many of the comic postcards that are so much a feature of every seaside town are printed in Holmfirth by J Bamforth & Company. The company was founded in 1870 by James Bamforth, an artist, who produced the backdrops for many of the cards and also for lantern slides.

Shortly after the turn of the century, the company was pioneering comedy films that were filmed around Holmfirth, using local people as actors. The company also began producing cards, often in sets of three, showing sentimental scenes and including the words of popular songs. During World War 1, cards featuring popular songs like *My*

Hero and *Goodbye Dolly Gray* sold well to people wanting to express their feelings to volunteers on the Western Front.

As these postcards declined in popularity, the company switched to comic postcards, many of which have become classics. In 1975, Kirklees Metropolitan Council was given a collection of Bamforth's postcards amassed by Major Robert W Scherer of Tampa, Florida. He was originally attracted to those cards depicting hymns and songs, but eventually expanded the collection to include all Bamforth's postcards.

Today Bamforth's still produce their comic cards, as well as fine greetings cards and calendars.

"LET'S GO NOW, HAROLD—YOU'VE EXPLORED EVERYTHING!"

TO THE CAVES →

A "BAMFORTH" COMIC

Holmfirth is home to J Bamforth & Company, the creators of the ubiquitous saucy seaside postcard. Basically inoffensive, the humour is traditionally based on the double entendre.

café **E** has appeared in nearly every episode of the TV series. For filming scenes inside the café, the wooden panelled interior has been reproduced in a studio set.

As you climb the steps **F**, there is a view of a cascade in the stream to the right. The houses above are built on the two-dwellings-on-four-storeys principle.

Another familiar landmark from the television series is the exterior of

the White Horse Inn **G**. Inside the inn are over 250 photographs of the stars, taken during filming. The inn makes an excellent halfway point on the walk for either a drink or a meal.

PEACE OF AMIENS

Above and to the right of the inn are buildings with weavers's windows on the upper storeys. Weaving was once a cottage industry in the area, but declined with the opening of large mills. A boost was given to sales of local cloth in the 19th century when a treaty was signed to mark the Peace of Amiens.

The tall, stone pillar **H**, known as T'owd Genn, was erected in 1802 to commemmorate the short-lived peace after the war with France. The pillar also bears a plaque showing the height reached by the water after the bursting of the Bilberry Dam.

◀ *As you descend once more towards Holmfirth there are striking views south into the valley and beyond.*

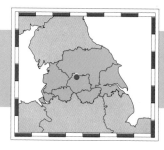

WEST YORKSHIRE

▲*Ilkley Moor, the ancient common, owned by Ilkley town, is an expanse of heather, bilberry, bracken, crag and open heath. Cladonia Impexa (left) is a hollow-stemmed lichen found on moors.*

A walk across open moorland on the edge of Ilkley town

Ilkley Moor is a nationally famous area of open moorland, its fame in part due to the Victorian popular song 'On Ilkla' Moor Baht 'At' — sometimes described as Yorkshire's national anthem.

The history of Ilkley **A** goes back to Iron Age times. Then it was a riverside settlement by a ford (Llecan) where the Romans built a camp (Olicana) to guard their road crossing of the Wharfe, downstream from the present 17th-century pack-horse bridge. Remains of the camp can be seen behind Ilkley's medieval church, which has three magnificent carved Anglo-Viking gravestone crosses inside the tower. The Tudor Manor house nearby contains many Roman archaeological finds. From the late 18th century onwards Ilkley enjoyed fame as a spa town.

THE SWASTIKA STONE

Ilkley College **B** was originally built in 1865 as White Wells Hydropathic Hotel. This architecturally outstanding building and park now houses the Ilkley Campus of Bradford and Ilkley Community College.

Further on the route is a narrow, wooded valley, Heber's Ghyll **C**, with ornamental paths and bridges, landscaped in typical late Victorian style. It takes its name from an old Ilkely family, the Hebers, of nearby Hollin Hall. The ghyll is noted for its ferns, oak and birch woods, and series of waterfalls. On the moor itself is the Swastika Stone **D**. The mysterious carving on this moorland boulder is in fact a 'folyfoot'; this is an ancient Indo-European symbol of eternal life. The carving has a modern replica alongside it. The original probably dates from some 2,500-3,000 years ago.

ARCHAEOLOGICAL RICHES

Ilkley Moor is particularly rich in archaeological remains, including literally scores of mysterious cup-and-ring-marked stones. It is a magnificent viewpoint across and into the centre of Wharfedale and the Yorkshire Dales National Park.

Further east is White Wells **E**, which was built as a small bathhouse in the 1760s by Squire Middleton of Ilkley. Situated over Ilkley Moor's most famous spring, it only took a few years before wealthy, gouty invalids were coming from all over England to be

---

<table>
<tr><td colspan="2">FACT FILE</td></tr>
<tr><td>✳</td><td>Ilkley, 10 miles (16 km) north of Bradford</td></tr>
<tr><td>OS</td><td>Pathfinder 671 (SE 04/14), grid reference SE 116477
miles 0 1 2 3 4 5 6 7 8 9 10 miles
kms 0 1 2 3 4 5 6 7 8 9 10 11 12 13 14 15 kms</td></tr>
<tr><td>🕐</td><td>2½ hours</td></tr>
<tr><td>▬</td><td>Can be very muddy in places with fairly steep climbs</td></tr>
<tr><td>P</td><td>Large central car park behind Brook Street, Ilkley</td></tr>
<tr><td>T</td><td>Frequent train services to Ilkley from Leeds or Bradford (Forster Square). Bus services from Leeds, Bradford, Skipton, Keighley</td></tr>
<tr><td>🏨 🍴</td><td>Ilkley has a wide choice of pubs and cafés</td></tr>
</table>

THE WALK

ILKLEY – ILKLEY MOOR

The walk begins in Ilkley **A**.

1 From the central car park or railway station cross to Brook Street (main shopping street). At the top of the road there is a T-junction with The Grove. Look for phone boxes on Wells Promenade (which leads off junction). Opposite are central gardens. Follow path to left of stream through gardens.

2 Cross to right-hand side of stream over bridge and exit from park at gate in top right-hand corner. Cross road and keep in same direction along Linnburn Mews, an unsurfaced road.

3 Go through gateway at road end, keep ahead past rear entrance to the college, through pedestrian gate right to path along the right bank of the stream along a shallow ravine.

4 Turn left away from the cattle grid and immediately right into road at front of Ilkley College **B**. Keep ahead.

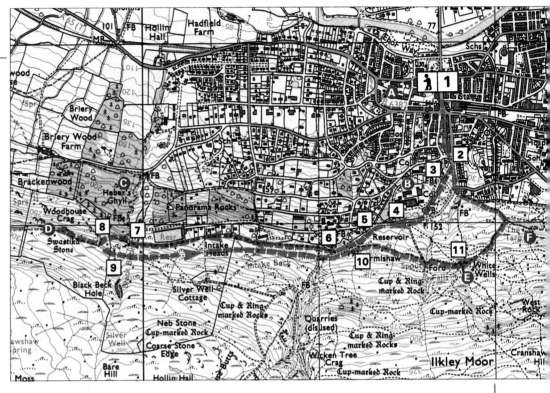

5 Turn left at the No Through Road sign and keep ahead up road towards moor.

6 Just by sheep warning sign, take grassy path right over bridge leading to track at moor edge above houses and reservoir.

7 Where path crosses bridge and dips to pedestrian gate on right, enter the wood called Heber's Ghyll **C**. Follow path along top of wood past stone shelter to gate back onto moor.

8 Face right (ignore gap stile) and take path forking left of stile through heather which dips over shallow stream and bears right. Join the main path and head for the Swastika Stone **D** on moor edge, enclosed behind tall metal fence. Retrace your steps.

9 Follow higher level path through bracken and heather which crosses two wooden footbridges. Keep ahead until path joins metalled road. Turn left downhill for about 220 yards (200 metres).

10 Look for narrow path on the right which starts by a large rowan tree. This follows shallow hollow parallel to road then swings right to meet track to White Wells **E**.

11 From White Wells take path on right below the upper Tarn **F** descending the moor to pass edge of the Tarn. Turn left along metalled track past paddling pool to Wells Promenade down to centre of Ilkley and start of walk.

carried by donkey from their Ilkley lodgings and plunged in the clear, icy waters. The Wells have been beautifully restored and are open at weekends and holiday times as a small museum and tea rooms.

Below White Wells are the Tarns **F**, which were landscaped from moorland pools to add to their picturesque effect. Much of the traditional moorland heather and bilberry, richly purple in late summer, has been lost through overgrazing and trampling. Over time the heather has been replaced by bracken and rough grass.

◄ *The tarns on Ilkley Moor were originally natural pools. They were landscaped during Victorian times.*

▼ *The inscription on the Swastika Stone states there is a similar carving at Tossene, Sweden and Mycene, Greece.*

ALONG THE TOWPATH

Walking by Britain's longest waterway to a wooded ravine

The walk goes along the towpath of the Leeds–Liverpool Canal, between Bingley and Saltaire, ascends to Shipley Glen at the edge of Baildon Moor, and leads back via a woodland path to the outskirts of Bingley and the canal-side path.

The Leeds-Liverpool Canal is Britain's longest inland waterway. Begun in 1770, it was soon superseded by the railway, but is much used today by pleasure craft. The start of the walk is on the towpath at Bingley, and begins with a diversion to visit two impressive pieces of canal engineering, the stepped Three Rise Locks and Five Rise

FACT FILE

- ☀ Bingley, between Bradford and Keighley

- ᴏˢ Pathfinders 671 (SE 04/14) and 682 (SE 03/13), grid reference SE 109391

  miles 0 1 2 3 4 5 6 7 8 9 10 miles
  kms 0 1 2 3 4 5 6 7 8 9 10 11 12 13 14 15 kms

- ◔ Allow 4 hours

- ▬ Good towpath, pavement and woodland path

- P Large 'pay and display' car park at start of walk

- T Frequent trains and buses from Bradford and Keighley

- 🍴 The Fisherman's pub by Dowley Gap; Boat House Café by river bridge at Saltaire; Old Glen House pub and tea gardens at Shipley Glen

- WC Near car park in Bingley. Also at Saltaire

- I Brackenhall Countryside Centre on Baildon Moor. Waterbus from Bingley to Shipley (summer only). Check (infrequent) opening times of the Glen Tramway

▲The Five-Rise at Bingley is the most elaborate of several 'staircase' locks on the Leeds-Liverpool Canal. Wood sage (left), which is found near here, can be used in brewing instead of hops.

Locks Ⓐ, where boats passing along the canal rise or fall 60 feet (18m) over a distance of 320 feet (98m).

From the locks, you retrace your steps past Bingley and continue on to Dowley Gap. Along the way are stops for the waterbus, which operates between Bingley and Shipley during the summer months. As an attractive alternative to the first part of the walk, you may prefer to catch the waterbus down to Saltaire and continue on foot from there.

At first, you pass a varied mixture of old and new warehouses and factories, but after about ½ mile (800m) it becomes a typical Pennine valley, with the river, canal, old turnpike road and railway running

THE WALK

BINGLEY – SALTAIRE – SHIPLEY GLEN

The walk starts from the car park off Ferncliffe Road between the railway station and the canal in Bingley.

➡️ Look for a gap in the wall with steps down to the canal towpath. Turn left and follow the towpath to the Three Rise Locks and the Five Rise Locks **A**. Retrace your steps past Bingley, and continue on to the bridge at Dowley Gap Locks by the canalside Fisherman's pub.

➡️ The towpath now

crosses the bridge (no. 2061) to the other side of the canal, and soon the canal is carried by an aqueduct across the River Aire **B**, before entering a wooded gorge. Continue

to Saltaire **C**, and leave the canal by turning right, over the road bridge in front of the mill buildings.

➡️ Walk up Victoria Road to see the mill, the church, the school and almshouses. Return to the bridge, cross it and enter Roberts Park.

➡️ Walk directly ahead through the right-hand end of the park, making a diversion to the centre of the park to see the statue of Sir Titus Salt **D**. Leave the far side of the park to cross the road to a roundabout and car park situated between Salt

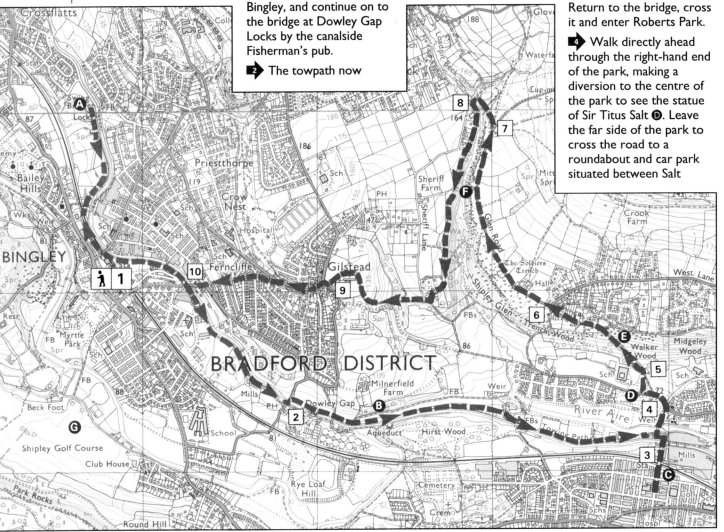

side by side. Yorkshire's wool trade was given a boost when the road from Keighley to Kendal was made into a turnpike in 1753. It became easier then for wool to be brought from the sheep-rearing areas of Westmorland to the industrial West Riding of Yorkshire.

Cross to the north side of the canal at the Dowley Gap

◀ *Sir Titus Salt's Hospital is a three-storey building, opened in 1858 as part of his new millworkers' community.*

Changeline Bridge. Soon after, an aqueduct carries the canal over the River Aire **B**. The wooded gorge through which both the river and canal flow makes an informal nature reserve, and it is hard to believe that you are so close to industry and housing. In places, the canal is lined with alder, rowan, hazel, beech, elder and sycamore, and the banks are thick with meadowsweet, ramsons, dog rose, yarrow and the conspicuous, rhubarb-like leaves of butterbur.

Grammar School and the playing field. Cross the roundabout towards the wooden buildings just ahead, at the foot of the Glen Tramway ⓔ.

5 Take the tramway to the top of the hill, or walk up the parallel path. Keep ahead along the suburban road, passing the Old Glen House on the left. The road now opens on to Brackenhall Green on Baildon Moor.

6 Continue on the road, or parallel path, passing the Brackenhall Countryside Centre on the right, followed by The Soldiers' Trench stone circle on the left. The way continues along the moor for about ½ mile (800m).

7 Take a signposted public footpath on the left, which goes between two bollards, downhill to a bridge over a stream. Cross over, and turn left to scramble up the steep path, joining a path on the left which goes along the wooded hillside.

8 Follow this woodland path along Shipley Glen ⓕ. After about ¾ mile (1,200m), when you reach a clear division in the path, with one path leading downhill and another curving uphill to the right, take the right-hand path and follow it round, joining a walled path after about 100 yards (90m). Turn right, and follow the path through a gate. About 20 yards (18m) after the gate, turn left along another walled path, dropping steeply through a wood to cross a stream. The path now goes uphill, ascending steps and curving round a garden on the left, before bearing left to join the road at Gilstead.

9 Turn right, and walk uphill for about 50 yards (45m), to the road junction. Turn left, past St Wilfrid's Church, and go downhill for about 200 yards (180m) before turning left down Ferncliffe Road. From here there are good views over Airedale ⓖ. Cross the road-bridge over the canal, and turn left to join the canal towpath.

10 Turn left to go under the bridge (no. 203). From here, it is a short distance back to the car park and station at Bingley, where the walk began.

At Saltaire ⓒ, Sir Titus Salt's great stone-built mill spans the canal. Opened with much ceremony on Sir Titus's 50th birthday, in 1853, it covers 25 acres (10 hectares), and has an ornamental chimney 250 feet (76m) high. It was built in a Venetian Gothic style, and intended to resemble an Italian palace.

◄*The stone lions outside Victoria Hall, made by T Milnes of London, are said to have originally been destined for Trafalgar Square, but were too small.*

The magnificent Congregational church opposite the mill, the burial place of Sir Titus and his family, is in the Italian Classical style. Further up the road to the south, the Victoria Hall has an impressive façade, with two stone lions at the front that were reputedly made for Trafalgar Square, but proved too small. Further on again are Sir Titus's almshouses and the hospital.

IMPRESSIVE MEMORIAL

Roberts Park, on the other side of the canal, is another example of early town planning. A splendid bronze statue of Sir Titus Salt ⓓ was erected in 1903 to celebrate the 100th anniversary of his birth. It stands on a plinth decorated with an angora goat and an alpaca, symbols of the wool industry on which the Victorian philanthropist built his very considerable success.

The route heads uphill to Shipley Glen on the edge of Baildon Moor. The Shipley Glen Tramway ⓔ saves some of the uphill climb. The open cars are hauled by cable 386 yards

▶ *This fine bronze statue of wool magnate Sir Titus Salt was constructed in his memory in Roberts Park.*

(353m) up a 1-in-12 incline, beneath overhanging trees. The tramway, built in the 19th century by a local man, Sam Wilson, was restored to operation in 1982 by the Bradford Trolleybus Association.

At the top of the slope is a small funfair, on the site of old Victorian pleasure grounds. A little further uphill you come to Brackenhall Green on Baildon Moor. Just past the

Countryside Centre are the remains of an ancient stone circle known as 'The Soldiers' Trench'. Originally, there were double rings of rough local stones. Some have been moved, but a careful reconstruction was made in the 1950s by members of the Bradford Archaeological Group. Boundary walls and neolithic corn-grinding stone querns have been discovered nearby.

Shipley Glen ●, to your left, is a typical Pennine gill, or ravine. On the moor there is a thin layer of acid soil between outcrops of bare millstone grit. It supports heather and bilberries, sheep's sorrel and clumps of soft rush, as well as various tough grasses, which are grazed by sheep and well trodden by people.

FRESH AIR

The rock used to be quarried as a building material. The algae and lichens that flourish on the exposed surfaces provide evidence of an

▲*Looking from the craggy outcrop of Shipley Glen, there are splendid views across the woods that cover Airedale.*

Saltaire

In the 1850s, wool magnate Sir Titus Salt decided to replace his four mills in Bradford with a large new one near Shipley, on the River Aire. He also planned a new community for his workers, with good housing and amenities, at a time when slums and exploitation were commonplace.

The result was Saltaire, a model industrial village and pioneering experiment in town planning. It was designed by the Bradford-based partnership of Lockwood and Mawson. The streets of solid, well-made houses all bear the first names of some of the important people of

Salt's mill was the centrepiece and raison d'être of his new community. Though vast, it was intended to be neither dark nor satanic.

the time; as well as Victoria and Albert, and Titus himself, two were named after Lockwood and Mawson and some were named after members of Salt's family — he was a devoted father of 11 children, and thus had plenty to choose from!

There was a hospital, almshouses with gardens, a factory school and a Congregational church. A park was provided, as well as a Club and Institute, now Victoria Hall, which was opened in 1871 as a social centre. The only thing missing was a pub; a strict non-conformist, Sir Titus would not allow alcohol anywhere in his new village. The wool magnate also played an active role in local politics and became Mayor of Bradford.

unpolluted atmosphere, despite the moor's proximity to industrial Yorkshire. Skylarks, lapwings and kestrels may be spotted, and magpies and crows nearer the woods.

In the mixed broadleaved woodland of the Glen there is a variety of plants, including wood avens, wood sage, marsh ragwort, goosegrass, self-heal and coltsfoot. Honeysuckle also trails along the ground. Beneath the trees in the oak and birch sections of the woodland are the acid-loving wavy hair-grass and creeping soft grass. There are many rabbits and squirrels in these parts.

VARIED LANDSCAPE

The woodland path brings you out into Gilstead, a suburb of Bingley. On the walk downhill towards the canal, there are good views over Airedale ●, where rural and industrial areas co-exist side by side — typical of West Yorkshire. Above and beyond the tops of the mill chimneys of Bingley, on the far side of the valley, there is an expanse of woodland and moors.

Along old trade routes and through a wooded valley

Heptonstall **A** is a historic village with a steep and winding cobbled main street. The earliest cottages date back to the 16th century. In the 17th and 18th centuries, when Heptonstall was at its peak as a textile community, some cottages were the homes of handloom weavers. These are distinguishable by their rows of upstairs windows, which allowed the weavers as much light as possible by which to work.

As you leave the village, you pass the parish church. The graves in the churchyard include that of David Hartley, who was hanged in York in

▲ *The view from Heptonstall Crags down to Calderside, which lies between Colden Water, the River Calder and Rochdale Canal. Yellow loosestrife (inset) grows along Hebaen Water.*

FACT FILE

✳ Heptonstall, 6½ miles (10.4km) west of Halifax, off the A646

▭ Pathfinder 690 (SD 82/92) or Outdoor Leisure Map 21, grid reference SD 987281

miles 0 1 2 3 4 5 6 7 8 9 10 miles
kms 0 1 2 3 4 5 6 7 8 9 10 11 12 13 14 15 kms

◕ Allow 2 hours

▬ Several steep ascents and descents through wooded ravines. Paths are well maintained but can be slippery or muddy. One river crossing on stepping stones. Particular care needed with children on top of Heptonstall Crags. Walking boots are essential

P Free car park at the start

T BR trains to Hebden Bridge on the main Manchester to Leeds line: an hourly bus service operates from the station to Heptonstall, Tel. (01422) 364467

▦ The Cross Inn and the White Lion, pub in Heptonstall

🍴 Café at Midgehole. The farm shop at Slack sells ice cream

WC Heptonstall and Midgehole

1770 for counterfeiting gold coins. Just beyond the church are the ruins of a 15th-century chapel dedicated to St Thomas à Becket, and next to them stands the village's Old Grammar School of 1642.

Heptonstall lies on an old route between Halifax and Burnley. The walled lane that leads out to Heptonstall Crags, Eaves Lane **B**, was once a route for packhorses and pedestrians. It passes through the South Field of a medieval twin-field farming system. The North Field lies beyond the church. Farmers were allotted strips within the fields, which were used alternately for growing corn, then left fallow. The terraced hummocks of the ridge-and-furrow strips are still visible in the lawns of the houses.

Heptonstall Crags **C** are an outcrop of gritstone. From this vantage point, there are excellent views down the Calder Valley. The stone tower visible from many locations is Stoodley Pike, erected to commemorate the Battle of Waterloo.

STEAM-POWERED MILLS

Down below is Colden Water. The area around here used to be owned by the monks of Fountains Abbey, and they built a number of small water-mills in the valley. The mills were later converted to steam power, but much of the early water engineering remains, now hidden in dense woods.

Murking Lane **D**, another walled

THE WALK

HEPTONSTALL – HEBDEN DALE

The walk starts in the free car park just off the main street in Heptonstall **A**.

1 From the car park exit, go diagonally right at the crossroads, along a lane signposted to the Museum. Go up the signposted steps to your right. Through a gate at the top are the church and the ruins of an earlier church. The Old Grammar School is on your right. Follow the path around to the left of the church. Leave the churchyard by a short path on your left, just beyond a tall brown obelisk. Turn right along the track. After 50 yards (45m), fork left. Fork right after another 50 yards (45m), signposted 'Calderdale Way', along the walled Eaves Lane **B**.

2 At the end of the lane, turn right, and make your way with care along the unfenced path at the top of Heptonstall Crags **C** to a

lane. Turn left, downhill, for about 100 yards (90m), then bear right along the waymarked Calderdale Way. The path soon joins a grassy, walled path (Murking Lane **D**) and continues along the hillside.

3 At the end of the track, turn sharp right on a field-edge path. Go through two small gates and a farmyard, and turn left along a track to the village of Slack.

4 Turn left down the road through the village. Before the road junction (the site of an old finger-post **E**), take a signposted path to your right, between houses, which opens into a walled lane. At the end of the lane, bear left and zigzag downhill through woods to Hebden Water.

5 Cross the stepping stones, and go left along the riverside path to Gibson Mill **F**. Return by the same path. Continue uphill, and bear right to

follow the river. After about ½ mile (800m), go up some steps. Continue along the path close to the river until you come to a bridge.

6 Turn right across the bridge, then bear left past the café at Midgehole. At a fork, bear right, uphill along a paved track. At a crossroads of tracks, turn left. Continue ahead, walking through the wooded hillside, until you come to a road.

7 Bear left and continue for about 50 yards (45m). Turn right up steps signposted to Heptonstall. At a road, turn right uphill to reach Heptonstall, and the car park.

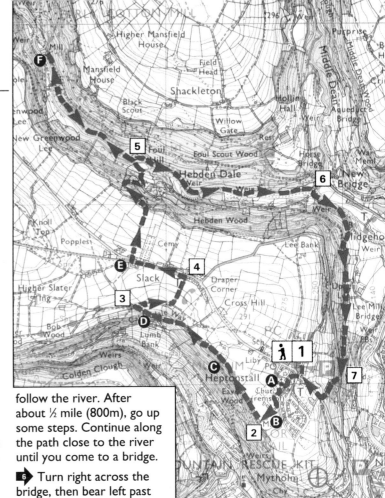

and partly paved lane, is followed for a time from Heptonstall Crags. It now forms part of a long-distance footpath, the Calderdale Way. There were many such routes between mills and villages, and, at the top of this lane, there is an intersection of five of these Pennine tracks.

The route goes through Slack,

where a 17th-century finger-post **E** indicates 'Burnly', an archaic spelling of Burnley. A green lane, lined with bilberry bushes, leads you to a wooded ravine, and you descend to Hebden Water. The woods are a botanist's paradise, with the flora including enchanter's nightshade, wood anemones, yellow pimpernel and pink campion. The treecreeper, a small, brown bird with a curved beak, probes the bark of trees here for insects.

You cross Hebden Water by stepping stones, known in these parts as 'hipping stones', and head upstream through pine woods to Gibson Mill **F**. The deserted mill is named after Abraham Gibson, a cotton spinner. The bridge here was once a tollbridge.

◀*You cross Hebden Water by stepping stones to walk alongside National Trust woodland to Gibson Mill.*

The route now heads back downstream. The woods are home to large wood ants, which make their nests out of the pine needles. As well as Scots pine, there are attractive mature trees including beech, birch and holly. In spring, the slopes are covered in bluebells, and you may also find wild hyacinth. At Midgehole, you cross the river by another old tollbridge, and head uphill along a track.

RADIATING LANES

At the top of the track, there are excellent views over the town of Hebden Bridge. Steep lanes radiate at all angles, and the houses are built tall and narrow in order to make the best use of scarce valley-bottom land. The colours of the stone houses and cottages reflect the hues of the surrounding hills. A further steep climb returns you to Heptonstall and the start.

These peaceful villages were once witness to a devastating local tragedy

A few miles north of Sheffield lie the villages of High and Low Bradfield situated between the Agden and Damflask Reservoirs. The Dale Dyke and Agden Dyke streams unite in Low Bradfield and form the River Loxley, which runs into Sheffield to join the River Don.

The grey stone church of St Nicholas **B** serves both villages and much of it dates from the 14th century. To the right of the churchyard entrance is the Watch House. Built in 1745, this housed guards whose function was to protect the dead from body-snatchers who sold the corpses to doctors for dissection.

There are spectacular views from the churchyard and from point **D** the Loxley Valley and the outskirts of Sheffield can be seen. This area was once full of mills, grinding sheds and cottages for workers in the steel industry.

Opposite the Old Horns Inn **E** are the village stocks. These were used to punish minor offenders, but it was far from a minor punishment — just a few hours clamped in the stocks left the culprit stiff, numb and unable to walk easily.

▲ *Low Bradfield is a peaceful Pennine village. Few signs remain of the havoc caused when water escaped from Agden Reservoir (left) and swept through the village. There are several hundred species of the common bramble (inset).*

These high Pennine villages, surrounded by natural beauty, were the scene of a disaster that took place in the last century.

THE DAM BURST

Local oral tradition still tells of the torrent of water that swept through the valley when Dale Dyke Dam burst in 1864. The then newly-built dam nestling in the valley below the moors was full for the first time. This massive feat of civil engineering was quite a crowd-puller until,

FACT FILE

⚹ Low Bradfield, 6 miles (9.6 km) north west of Sheffield

🚗 Pathfinder 726 (SK 29/39), grid reference SK 262919

miles 0 1 2 3 4 5 6 7 8 9 10 miles
kms 0 1 2 3 4 5 6 7 8 9 10 11 12 13 14 15 kms

◔ Allow 3 hours

▬ There is quite a steep climb from Low Bradfield to viewpoint **C**

🍴 Low Bradfield: the Plough Inn; shop, toilets, picnic site near the river. High Bradfield: Old Horns Inn

WC

T Bus service to Sheffield

THE WALK

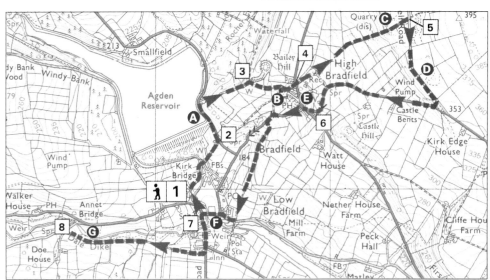

LOW BRADFIELD – HIGH BRADFIELD

*The walk begins at the car park near Kirk Bridge, by Agden Reservoir **A**.*

1 From the car park entrance, turn back between stone walls on a track marked 'Unsuitable for Motors'. Follow the flagged path to the river, ignore the first footbridge and follow the flagged path marked 'Public footpath to High Bradfield' beside the stream and cross the second footbridge. Climb the steps to a stile set in the wall, turn left and fork right up five steps. The path continues with a drystone wall on your right to a road.

2 Turn left for 300 yards (270 metres) and turn right up a signposted footpath to Bailey Hill shortly after reaching Agden Reservoir. The path then climbs steeply, with a stone wall on your right.

3 Turn right over a wooden stile and keep the wire fence on your right as you walk towards Bradfield Church **B** . The path passes through two small gates and the churchyard, leading to a stile beside the Watch House. Turn left up Jane Street.

4 Cross straight over the road to a stone stile to the left of a trough. Pass a farm on your right and continue, keeping a stone wall on your right. Cross the next field to a squeeze stile beside a gate at the field corner, then continue with a wall on your right to the crest of the hillside. At viewpoint **C** pause and look back at the view. Continue to the stile on to the road to the left of the metal gate.

5 Turn right along the road. After about 300 yards (270 metres) there is an excellent view towards the outskirts of Sheffield from viewpoint **D** . Turn sharp right at the road junction and descend to High Bradfield.

6 Fork right on the road signposted to Low Bradfield and at the next junction by the Old Horns Inn **E** continue towards Low Bradfield. After about 100 yards (90 metres) take the path signposted to Low Bradfield over stone steps set in a wall. Continue with the wall on your left. Yellow arrows indicate the route over stiles. Descend the hillside to a set of stone steps that lead down to the road. Turn right to the junction and fork left on Smithy Bridge Road in Low Bradfield **F** . Cross over the bridge and turn left over the next bridge. (If you wish to return to the car park now turn right and right again along the area known as The Sands).

7 Walk straight on to the Plough Inn. Turn right on the footpath that leads to a gate near a house, then continue straight ahead along the valley **G** . Pass to the right of a gate and follow the fence on your left to a stone stile. The path then continues to a stile which leads on to a road.

8 Return to the Plough Inn and turn left down to the bridge. At the road junction keep straight ahead and take the first right back to the car park along The Sands, and to the start of the walk.

one day, cracks were discovered in the dam wall. It was nearly mid-night when the dam burst and 90 per cent of the 712 million gallons (3,500 million litres) of water escaped. There were heavy casualties; the route the water took down to Low Bradfield and Sheffield can still be traced on the landscape.

Some three minutes after the dam burst a 50-feet (15-metres) high wall of water hit Low Bradfield **F** . The newly-built Wesleyan School, corn mill, smithy and a number of cottages simply disappeared under the force of the water. A 70-feet (15-metres) wall of water ran along this narrow valley.

Today Dale Dyke Reservoir can be seen from viewpoint **C** . Agden Reservoir **A**, completed in 1869, has a capacity of 629 million gallons (3,000 million litres). Its embankment is 1,500 feet (450 metres) across and 90 feet (27 metres) high.

High Bradfield's Watch House still overlooks the churchyard, but the occupants no longer have to prevent freshly-buried corpses from being unearthed and sold to doctors for medical research.

WENTWORTH WOODHOUSE

17

From the iron works to the homes of the earls who owned them

▲ *Wentworth was built in 1734 by the first Marquis of Rockingham, William Watson Wentworth. The pipistrelle bat (right) is the smallest in Britain, as well as the most widespread and abundant.*

The 18th century saw the rapid development of iron and coal mining around Elsecar, due to the entrepreneurial activities of the Earls Fitzwilliam, who owned the massive ancestral home of the Marquis of Rockingham. This walk

passes through the gentle, undulating, wooded countryside between the industrial South Yorkshire towns of Rotherham and Barnsley. As it does so, it explores the Wentworth Woodhouse estate. It takes in the contrast of the elegant landscaped parkland, beautiful monuments and Palladian mansion, with the small mining community that created the wealth to sustain them.

Elsecar, now a most attractive conservation area and important industrial heritage site, was developed in the 18th and 19th centuries by the Earls Fitzwilliam of Wentworth Woodhouse as a coal-mining and iron-working community. In 1795, Elsecar iron works

◄ *Across fields from Elsecar, the 180-foot (55-metre) spire of Wentworth's neo-Gothic church comes into view.*

FACT FILE

✳ Elsecar, 6 miles (9.6 km) south-east of Barnsley

▭ Pathfinders 726 (SK 29/39) and 727 (SK 49/59), grid reference SK 999383

miles 0 1 2 3 4 5 6 7 8 9 10 miles
kms 0 1 2 3 4 5 6 7 8 9 10 11 12 13 14 15 kms

◷ 4 hours

▬ Clear, easy tracks for most of the route

P Elsecar; turn left at the Market Inn

T Regular trains and buses from Barnsley and Sheffield

▦ Pubs in Elsecar and pubs and cafés in Wentworth

THE WALK

ELSECAR – NETHER HAUGH

The walk starts from the car park beyond the Market Inn.

1 Turn right down the lane to the Market Inn. Turn right down Forge Lane past a long row of early 19th-century workshops **A**. Take the right-hand fork and then almost immediately take the path on the left into Kings Wood. On entering the wood take the left fork and continue straight ahead. At second fork in wood, bear right to a gate and wooden stile.

2 Go over the stile and bear left across the field to a fence and hedge opposite. Follow the hedge uphill to a gate and stile. Keep alongside the fence and hedge, descending slowly, and turn left to join an enclosed track. Continue along the track, turn right past a joiners' yard and workshop to join a road.

Follow the road left into Wentworth village.

3 Walk straight ahead crossing the main road and continue up Church Field Lane. Turn left through a gateway along the church drive which passes between the two churches **B** and continues to a road.

4 At the road turn left to the War Memorial and road

junction and then bear right following the park wall to reach the entrance of Wentworth Woodhouse.

5 Turn right down the main drive through the parkland and past a cattle grid. Where the main drive swings sharply right to the house **C**, continue straight ahead following the line of the fence to join a tarmac track.

6 Continue for 1 mile (1.6 km) along the track through woods, to where the lakes and Keppel's column come into view **D**. About 200 yards (180 metres) from a junction on the right, find a new stile on the left and follow a farm track. Cross track past a

group of trees before veering right at an angle of 45°, using the village ahead as a bearing. Descend across the field down to a new stile and new wooden bridge.

7 Walk up the field by the side of the hedge and look for a stile on the right from where the Wentworth Mausoleum **E** can be seen. Go through the next field and look for a second stile by the side of a grey cottage. Turn left along the lane.

8 At the road turn left to a junction and then left again along Cortworth Lane. Go past the lodge on the left and, just after the road narrows, look for a footpath sign on the right.

9 Follow the hedge up the field, and go through

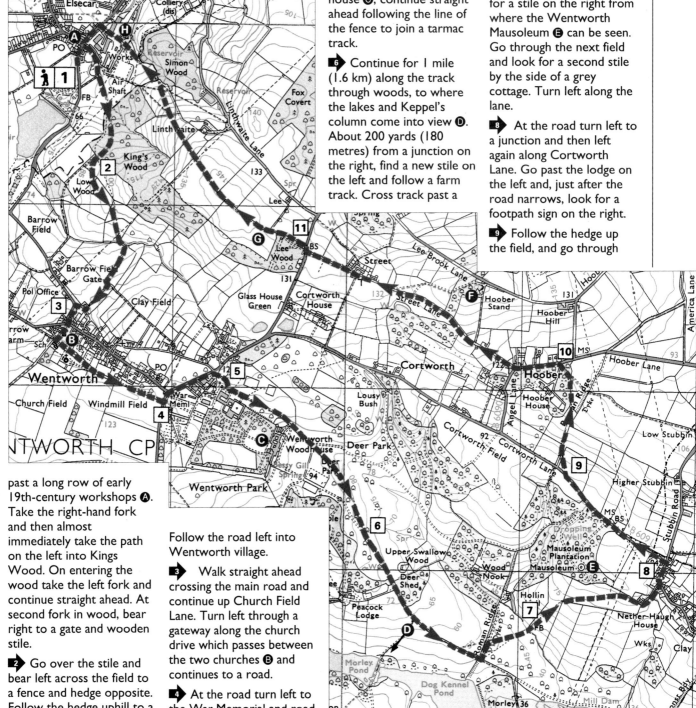

the gap at the top. Cross the next field to a cottage and stile. Over the stile continue straight ahead and take the next stile on the left. Follow the path through the wood to a stile and the road.

10 Follow the road for about 200 yards (180 metres) to where it swings sharply to the left and take the signed track branching on the right. Walk along the track past Hoober Stand **F**. The track becomes a lane at the hamlet of Street and emerges at Coaley Lane. At the road junction, cross over. Almost opposite take the signed steps on the right.

11 Follow the footpath past the Needles Eye **G** on the left and slowly descend down the ridge to a stile.

At the stile swing right and then drop down to Elsecar passing the Newcomen engine **H** on your left. At the road turn left to the Market Inn and then continue straight ahead to the car park and the start of the walk.

were completed, using ironstone from Tankersley Park 2 miles (3.2 km) away. In the same year, the shaft for the Elsecar New Colliery was sunk, to meet the increased demand for coal. The Newcomen Engine **H** was installed at the pit-head to pump water out of the mine.

Elsecar became the focus for a number of collieries, as well as a large engineering shop and tar distillery. The town developed as an important industrial centre linked to the Dearne and Dove canal and later the railway, with the Earls

▲*In the heart of Wentworth village is the aptly-named Paradise Square. One of the two churches (right) in the village is partially ruined. The 17th-century façade of the nave and the medieval west tower, however, are still standing.*

Fitzwilliam building their own private station. The trains entered an enclosed building that had offices built above. The earls were also responsible for building most of the miners' and foundry workers' cottages. These were constructed to a very high standard for that period, being well-built, four-roomed houses, each of which had a small garden and shared privy. There is a fascinating heritage trail around the town which is well worth exploring.

WORKSHOPS

Forge Lane passes alongside some fine 19th-century workshops **A** built by the fifth Earl between 1850-60 to serve all his coalmining, iron-making and engineering enterprises.

◀*The grounds of Wentworth Woodhouse contain lush green parkland, where cattle can graze.*

These are, in fact, only a fraction of the full number of Elsecar workshops. They were originally the brain-child of John Hartop, then manager of Elsecar iron works. The entire site is now owned by the Metropolitan Borough Council of Barnsley who have renovated and developed a Heritage Centre and Technology Museum there.

In Wentworth, there are two churches **B**. Holy Trinity was designed by J L Pearson and built between 1875 and 1877 by the sixth Earl Fitzwilliam in memory of his late father, the fifth Earl.

The medieval church dates back to before 1235, and has been rebuilt

twice, in 1491 and in 1684. The medieval west tower and the elegant 17th-century façade of the nave still stand next to Wentworth Chapel, the chancel and north chapel of the old church. The old church was extensively restored between 1975-86 by the Redundant Churches Fund and is now open to

▲In the 19th century, woodwork and metalwork repairs were carried out in these workshops on Forge Lane.

the public on summer Sunday afternoons, or at other times by request. Inside, there are many fine monuments to the Wentworth family. These date back as far as 1460, with the fine alabaster figures of Sir Gascoyne and his wife. Visitors also have the opportunity of visiting the Fitzwilliam vaults under the chapel, where eight members of the family are buried.

Wentworth Woodhouse ● stands as a magnificent symbol of the great power and vast wealth of the 18th-century aristocracy. From the footpath you can see its massive 600-foot (180-metre) east façade — in comparison, the famous Mall façade of Buckingham Palace is only 352 feet (99 metres). Each of the ranges on either side of the colonnaded centre makes a large country house in its own right. Across the valley, on the horizon above the lakes, is Keppel's column ●, a magnificent 115-foot (35-metre) monument designed by John Carr. It was built to commemorate the acquittal of Lord Rockingham's friend Admiral Keppel, who was court-martialled for failing to beat the French in the battle of 1778 in the American War of Independence.

CORINTHIAN COLUMNS

The Wentworth Mausoleum ●, was built over a period of three years by 10 men. It rises in three sections. The enclosed ground floor is surmounted by colonnades, with an arcade of Corinthian columns. The third section is a cupola, which once held a life-sized statue of the Marquis and

The Newcomen Engine

Thomas Newcomen, a Cornishman and perhaps one of the world's least known but greatest engineers, invented the atmospheric engine. The first one was built in 1712 to drain the Cornish tin mines. Newcomen's engine played an important part in quickening the pace of industrial developments in the 18th century. For a long time, it was the only successful and efficient means of draining mines.

The Newcomen-type engine in Elsecar was built in 1795 by John Bargh of Chesterfield to drain the Earl Fitzwilliam New Colliery Mine that was opened that year. This great 48-inch (1.2-metre) cylinder engine cost £167 19s 3d to build, and had a horse power of 13.16. It was capable of draining 400 gallons (1818 litres) of water per minute.

As you stand by where the engine is housed, you can still see the arms of the great rocking engine appearing from an upper storey window. The original wooden beam, with its chains connected to the piston and pump, were replaced in 1836 by the existing 24-foot (7.3-metre) iron one, which had to be cast in two sections. In 1836 the (incorrect) 1787 datestone was also added.

The Elsecar Newcomen engine is the last surviving Newcomen beam engine in the entire world that is still in situ. It was in regular operation until 1923 and was last used in 1928, when it was called into service during a major flood that put the more modern electrical equipment completely out of action!

The Elsecar Newcomen engine is the only beam engine in the world that is still standing on the site where it was once in use.

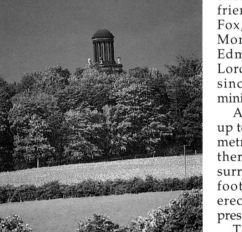

▲Peeping through trees across a field is Wentworth Mausoleum, a memorial to the second Marquis of Rockingham.

busts of eight of his great political friends: Admiral Keppel, Charles Fox, Sir George Savile, Frederick Montagu, The Duke of Portand, Edmund Burke, Edmund Lee and Lord John Cavendish. These have since had to be removed due to mining subsidence.

A footpath leads from the track up to Hoober Stand ●, 518 feet (158 metres) above sea level. From here, there are splendid views over the surrounding countryside. The 100-foot (30-metre) monument was erected to commemorate the suppression of the Jacobite rebellion.

The Needle's Eye ● was built in 1780, supposedly in response to a wager by the Marquis of Rockingham that a horse and carriage should be driven through the eye of a needle. It consists of a pyramid tower surmounted by a stone urn and pierced by a carriageway.

TO THE GRINDSTONE

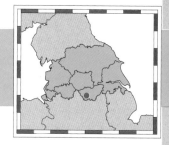

18

Through the valley where Sheffield's cutlery industry began

The abundance of readily available water power laid the foundations of Sheffield's traditional metal industries. By the end of the 18th century, the city's five rivers were lined by cutlery and scythe manufacturers, grinding wheels, forges and rolling mills, as well as corn, paper and snuff mills. In the 1770s there were over 150 water-powered workshops, with 20 mills sited along a 3 mile (4.8 km) stretch of the River Rivelin alone.

MINERAL DEPOSITS

A little way up the valley, just beyond an attractive stone bridge, is the site of Roscoe Wheel **A**. The weir here is unusual in that it is made up of three shallow-sloped gradients. A little further along is the now overgrown Holme Head Dam **B**, full of young oak and sycamore trees, and woodland birds such as the coal, great and blue tits. Look for the iron ochre spring, which is bright orange in colour from the iron minerals deposited in the water. It rises in the Ringinglow coal seams above.

Just before you reach the road is Nethercut Wheel **C**. It was the last

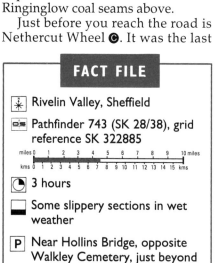

FACT FILE

- ✳ Rivelin Valley, Sheffield
- ▭ Pathfinder 743 (SK 28/38), grid reference SK 322885

  miles 0 1 2 3 4 5 6 7 8 9 10 miles
  kms 0 1 2 3 4 5 6 7 8 9 10 11 12 13 14 15 kms

- ◔ 3 hours
- ▭ Some slippery sections in wet weather
- P Near Hollins Bridge, opposite Walkley Cemetery, just beyond Walkley Bank Road
- T Bus no. 54 from Hillsborough, Tel. (01709) 515151 for times
- ▤ The Bell Hagg pub

▲ The site where Uppercut Wheel was housed was once the scene of an industrial dispute known as a 'rattening'. The bank vole (left) feeds on mushrooms and blackberries.

wheel to work in the valley and was involved in finishing scythes. It stopped in 1934. All the water control mechanisms are well-preserved and you can still pick out the weir and wheel pit. It was first recorded as Marrshal Wheel in 1726 and used for producing cutlery during the 19th century.

In 1874, there was dispute known as a 'rattening'. These disputes were particularly prevalent during the early part of the 19th century, when many of the small cutlery unions or trade societies sought to enforce their authority by terrorism, destroying or removing offenders' tools and equipment. By the mid-19th century, there were several assassination attempts and some factories were even blown up. These incidents became known as the Sheffield Outrages and forced a government investigation in 1867.

Across the road is Uppercut Wheel **D**, which was the site of another 'rattening' incident in 1850. The outline of the wheel building is exceptionally clear, though the wheel pit is now choked with

THE WALK

RIVELIN VALLEY

The walk starts at Rivelin Valley Road (A 6101), just beyond Walkley Bank Road.

1 Cross bridge and turn left following a riverside path upstream. Walk past paddling pools and on through a children's play area (once the site of Spooner Dam).

2 Continue over a small bridge. Turn right, passing allotments on the left, and a concrete footbridge and a stone bridge on the right. This path takes you past the site of Roscoe Wheel **A** and Holme Head Dam **B**. Where the path forks, turn right to a large mill pond and Nethercut Wheel **C** and the road.

3 Cross the road and go past the public toilets. Just before the bridge go down the steps to rejoin the riverside path and reach Uppercut Wheel **D**.

4 Continue along a narrow path between the river and a mill-race (stream) to a small concrete bridge crossing the river. Head straight towards the large mill pond ahead by Round Dam **E** and follow the path skirting its edge.

5 This next section takes nearly as long as all the walk so far. The path continues up the valley, passing several old mill sites and the largest dam **F** in the valley. Ignore the many minor paths — if in doubt, always take the broader track. After about 20 minutes, you will pass an open, grassy clearing on the right. Take right-hand fork marked 'Nature Trail'. Go past a second grassy clearing in the trees and take another right-hand fork uphill to a road.

6 Walk straight ahead through the lay-by and leave by a broad track, passing the site of Second Coppice Wheel **G** to a small stone bridge by Upper Coppice Wheel **H**.

7 At the bridge, swing sharp left across the river and follow the path downstream for a short stretch before climbing uphill to join a road.

8 Ignore the footpath sign directly opposite; instead, walk 30 yards (27 metres) left along the road. Cross over to a Public Byway sign pointing up a long, stony track.

9 Continue along the walled track climbing steadily towards a house on the horizon. Just before this house, turn left along a narrow path at a stone gatepost.

10 Turn right up road and cross over to a small metal gate in wall. Follow the path, which zigzags down the hill to bottom storey of the Bell Hagg pub. Turn left at the Public Footpath sign and down to a stone stile. Over the stile, swing right to a gate.

11 Cross the next field heading towards another gateway and stile. Over the stile, turn left immediately. Keeping the wall on your left, go downhill. Two walls cross your route to join the one on your left. At the second of these, a stone stile in the left-hand corner leads onto a lane.

12 Turn right down lane, passing some cottages on the left. Pass farm building on right and take footpath on left. After only 20 yards (18 metres), turn hard right at a low, square post bearing the 'Nature Trail' sign — this is easy to miss, so start looking for it in the vegetation as soon as you pass through the wooden barriers.

13 The path gradually ascends through another

set of wooden barriers. When the track forks, bear left. Soon it begins to descend, finally emerging at the road and the public toilets. Cross the road and, where the path forks, take the path on the right back to the bridge and start of the walk.

rubble. In 1794, this powered eight troughs and employed 13 men. The path runs alongside a conduit that was linked to the Hind Wheel Dam or Round Dam **E**. This has recently been dredged. The earliest recorded rental of the Hind Wheel goes back as far as 1581.

The Wolf Wheel was fed by the largest dam in the valley, a long thin dam **F**, which has now been dredged for fishing. In 1830, Wolf Dam worked a huge iron wheel that powered 19 cutlers' troughs.

By a small bridge, a waterfall once used as a weir by a mill here cascades down on the right. In 1814, the mill was a paper mill and today it is hard to imagine that it was once surrounded by two drying houses, a rope shed, dwelling, stable, rolling house, store, cowhouse and other outbuildings. Further on, there are two more wheel sites, **G** and **H**.

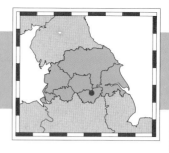

◀ *From the path above Hooton Pagnell's war memorial, there is a good view west over the village. Red bartsia (inset), a semi-parasitic plant, can be seen growing beside Narrow Balk.*

A flight of 13 steps leads to the 11th-century All Saints' Church ❸, the key to which is available from a nearby house. Several Norman features survive, including a massive arch and traces of herring-bone masonry. There is an ancient font and a fine, 18th-century marquetry pulpit. The most unusual feature is the Victorian carillon, which plays a different tune every day of the week, every three hours.

PICTURESQUE VILLAGE

The route through the village leads past picturesque limestone cottages. Hooton Pagnell's outward appear-ance has changed little since the Middle Ages. From the remains of the 13th-century butter cross there is a magnificent view westward towards the Pennines. The elegant Frickley Hall stands in its park about a mile (1.6km) across the green fields to the west, while South Elmsall Colliery looms to the north-west. Almost directly beneath the cross is the village pound, a stone-walled enclosure for stray cattle.

You leave the village along a lane called Narrow Balk ❹ ('balk' is a local name for a lane wide enough for farm carts), which follows the line of the medieval strip fields. The tall hedgerows are a haven for a pro-liferation of wild flowers, including

Very different country houses, each in a picturesque village

The limestone cottages and farms of Hooton Pagnell are perched on a hillside. One of the prettiest estate villages in the area, it has won the 'Best Kept Village' competition three times. A first view of it from the cricket ground, where this walk begins, takes in both medieval Hooton Pagnell Hall ❹ and a Tudor tithe barn.

The black sheep that are often to be found grazing in the field by the pitch complete the picture. The original flock was brought from St Kilda, in the Outer Hebrides, and their wool goes to make suits.

DISTANT IMPRESSION

The hall is not open to the general public, but an excellent impression of it can be obtained from the gate-way, through which you can see a wing of the house with charming oriel windows and a porch. In Norman times, Ralph de Pagnel was lord of the manor, and he added his name to the village, which was listed as 'Hotone' (the town on the hill) in the *Domesday Book*.

The hall was also the home of the Luttrell family, who, in 1340, commissioned the *Luttrell Psalters*, a unique illuminated medieval manuscript that provides a fine illustration of 14th-century life.

FACT FILE

❋ Hooton Pagnell, 6 miles (9.6km) north-west of Doncaster, on the B6422

🗺 Pathfinder 716 (SE 40/50), grid reference SE 485077

miles 0 1 2 3 4 5 6 7 8 9 10 miles
kms 0 1 2 3 4 5 6 7 8 9 10 11 12 13 14 15 kms

🕐 Allow at least 2½ hours

▬ Easy walking on field paths and lanes

🅿 Roadside parking near the start

🍴 Teas and light refreshments at Hooton Pagnell's post office, Tel. (01977) 643604

Ⓣ Buses from Doncaster, Tel. (0114) 276 8688

🏰 Brodsworth Hall opens Tues-Sun, and Bank Holidays, grounds 12-6pm, house 1-5pm, admission charge. Tel. English Heritage on (01302) 722598 for details

▼ *Hooton Pagnell has some attractive cottages built from the local limestone.*

THE WALK

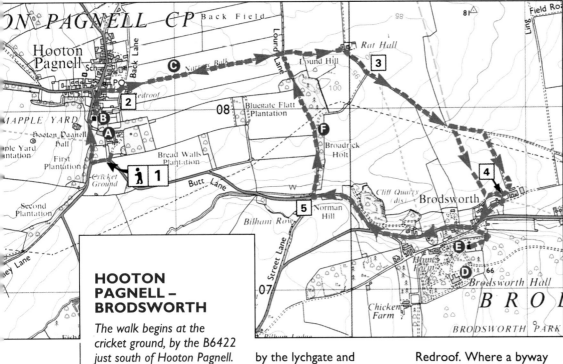

HOOTON PAGNELL – BRODSWORTH

The walk begins at the cricket ground, by the B6422 just south of Hooton Pagnell.

1 Facing the cricket ground, turn left. Follow the high wall on your left for a short distance, to view the tithe barn through the lane entrance. Return to the road junction and turn right, passing the entrance to Hooton Pagnell Hall **A** on your right. Climb the steps up to All Saints' Church **B**. Leave by the lychgate and continue down the lane, passing the butter cross on your left. Just beyond Ivy Cottage on your right, follow a signposted footpath up a drive and on along an avenue of beech trees, to a junction.

2 Cross the lane and take the public footpath (Narrow Balk **C**) to the left of a house called Redroof. Where a byway crosses, go ahead along a bridleway, keeping left of the hedge. At Rat Hall farm, follow the drive to the right of the house, then turn right on the bridleway.

3 Where the main track veers right, take the bridleway to the left. Follow it downhill between hedges. Eventually it runs between open fields. Just beyond this point, the public footpath (not signposted) crosses an open field on your right. (If this is ploughed or planted over, continue to the next hedge on your right and follow the cart track to its left, uphill towards the barns. Turn right just before the barns, and pass a cottage on the right.)

4 Turn right (or left if you have come the longer way) down a grassy lane, then right on a tarmac lane. Go downhill, across the B6422, and through the stone gateposts opposite, to the estate of Brodsworth Hall **D**. Follow the signposted lane to the church **E**. Return down the lane and rejoin the B6422. Turn left. The road curves right, then left (take care here, as there is no pavement).

5 By a bus shelter, turn right on a signposted path uphill. Beyond the site of the old cross **F**, fork left. The path leaves the trees, and goes down to the junction with Narrow Balk. Turn left and retrace your steps to the start.

dog rose, scabious and knapweed.

Brodsworth lies in a peaceful valley. Hidden among the trees on the hillside is Brodsworth Hall **D**, which has been described as 'the most complete example of a Victorian country house in England'. The Old Hall in the park was the home of the Thellussons, a French Huguenot family. They came to England in 1750, and created a family fortune based on banking. Charles Sabine Thellusson had the present hall built in the 1860s.

The Church of St Michael and All Angels **E** stands on a nearby hillside in a peaceful woodland setting. It contains memorials to the Thellussons, and many medieval features. Subsidence caused by mining has taken its toll on the

▼*The crack running up the tower of St Michael and All Angels' Church is a result of subsidence caused by mining.*

church, which for many years stood swathed in scaffolding. One phase of restoration by British Coal is now complete, though the interior walls are still undergoing repair.

BROADRICK HOLT

You return to Narrow Balk and Hooton Pagnell on a pleasant byway alongside the trees of Broadrick Holt. Marked on the map is the site of an ancient cross **F**, though you will not find any trace of it among the dense undergrowth; it has been removed for safekeeping and is awaiting restoration locally. The cross is believed to have been erected in the 14th or 15th century, on a pilgrim route to St Helen's Spring and Chapel, near Barnburgh, some 3 miles (4.8km) to the south.

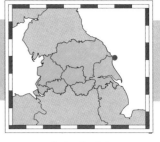

auctions were often held on the shore and the catch sent to Hull. The lifeboat station was built in 1871. Its occupants helped save over 108 lives until 1938, when the building became a seascout base.

The highest point between Bridlington and Flamborough takes its name from the warning beacon that was regularly lit on the spot. In

◀ *White-capped waves pound the coastline where fishing (below left) and common fleabane (below) both flourish.*

A walk around an historic headland and smugglers' haunts

Flamborough Head is a massive chalk headland on the east Humberside coast that juts far out into the North Sea, forming one of the most dramatic coastal features of the British Isles. Cliffs up to 400 feet (120 metres) high in places have been gouged and carved by the wild North Sea into a series of often fan-tastic shapes, with caves, arches, stacks and even blow-holes all around the headland, but particularly impressive around the Head itself by the famous lighthouse **Ⓚ**.

COLOURFUL PAST

Flamborough Head also has its place in history, being the site of many tragic shipwrecks and the haunt of smugglers, who used the little 'landings' or coves to bring in their illicit booty. It is also the site of the first sea battle won by the embryonic American Navy in the late-18th century.

As a breeding ground for many rare seabirds, it is also a nature reserve of national importance. For all these reasons, Flamborough Head now has special protection as one of Britain's Heritage Coasts.

With its small sandy beach beneath the cliffs, South Landing **Ⓐ** is typical of the small coves found along this coastline. On the other side of the headland is North Landing **Ⓙ** where, in the old days, fishermen would keep their boats, deciding from day to day which one to sail, depending on the winds.

Flamborough Head was a significant port between the 14th and 16th centuries, and even in the 19th century some 80 fishing boats, known as 'cobles', were based here. Fish

FACT FILE

✳	Flamborough Head, Humberside
🖼	Pathfinder 646 (TA 26/27), grid reference TA 230695

miles 0   1   2   3   4   5   6   7   8   9   10 miles
kms 0 1 2 3 4 5 6 7 8 9 10 11 12 13 14 15 kms

◔	Allow 3¹/₂–4 hours
▬	Fairly easy walking along field and clifftop paths, but a number of short, steep stretches on the cliff path; can be slippery in wet weather. Keep children under control and well away from the cliff edges, which can be unstable
P	Car park at Heritage Coast Information Centre at South Landing, ¹/₂ mile (800 metres) south of Flamborough village
T	Regular bus service from Bridlington to Flamborough village. Minibus service on summer Sundays
🍴 WC 🏛	Picnic site and toilets at Heritage Centre. Cafés at North Landing, Flamborough Lighthouse and Flamborough village. Pubs in the village

THE WALK

FLAMBOROUGH – FLAMBOROUGH HEAD

The walk begins outside the Heritage Centre (South Landing) **Ⓐ**.

1 Walk down the lane towards South Landing beach **Ⓐ**.

2 After passing the Old Lifeboat House, take the steep steps on the right. From the summit follow the coastal path over Beacon Hill **Ⓑ**.

3 Just over the brow of Beacon Hill, from which you can clearly see Danes Dyke **Ⓒ**, take the signposted footpath on the right to Flamborough village. The path follows a fence by a field to join a track. Continue over two stiles by gates and pass the side of a farm towards the village.

4 Bear right along West Street, which becomes Butler Lane. At T-junction turn right past the church-yard but go through the pedestrian gate on the left to the church **Ⓓ** entrance.

5 Continue along the path through the churchyard to the road, then turn right to the junction. Follow Tower Road past the peel tower **Ⓔ** in field on left to the centre of the village **Ⓕ**. At the crossroads continue ahead past the granite monument and along Chapel Street, which becomes Woodcock Road.

6 After last bungalow on the left-hand side (just past Beech Avenue), look for a stile and footpath sign on the left. Follow the waymarked path with a fence and ditch on the left for 250 yards (225 metres), then turn left between fences. After 50 yards (45 metres) turn right to cross a stile. Walk beside hedge on right, crossing two more stiles and passing a large caravan site in a field on the right.

7 The footpath joins the clifftop path at a stile east of Bempton Cliffs **Ⓖ**. Turn right and follow the footpath that leads towards Thornwick Bay **Ⓗ**.

8 Keep to the main path along the cliff. Descend the steps on left, cross a footbridge and ascend more steps ahead (leading to a café). At a rough track, 100 yards (90 metres) before a tarmac road, descend steps on left to cross another gully. Walk round the headland towards North Landing.

9 Descend and reclimb another steep ravine to emerge at North Landing **Ⓙ**.

10 Walk to the left side of the café and gift shop to rejoin the cliff path leading past a cottage towards Flamborough Lighthouse **Ⓚ**.

11 Keep to the cliff path beside the lighthouse, making for the fog signalling station. Bear right to take the clifftop path along the headland **Ⓛ** back towards South Landing.

12 Just before reaching South Landing, the path swings abruptly right above a small wooded valley. Steps on the left lead down to the beach; otherwise keep right to follow the gravel path to the head of the little valley and South Landing picnic site.

13 Turn left over a footbridge and up the path that leads directly into the picnic area and car park.

1588, the year of the Spanish Armada, there were three beacons on the headland — one on Beacon Hill **Ⓑ**, one on the headland itself and a third on the north end of Danes Dyke **Ⓒ**.

ANCIENT DEFENCES

The dyke, an old defensive structure, stretches for 2¹⁄₂ miles (3.7 km), bisecting the headland with ramparts 16 feet (4.5 metres) high and a ditch 20 feet (6 metres) wide and 60 feet (18 metres) deep. Its name is misleading, as it long pre-dates the Danish invasions. It actually goes back to the Iron Age, some time between 300 BC and AD 100, having been built by people whose only tools were flint weapons. It was a defensive fortification, designed to make the entire headland impregnable by sea or land. It is now a nature reserve.

Flamborough church **Ⓓ** dates from Norman times and is dedicated to St Oswald, early Christian king of Northumbria and patron saint of

◀ *Flamborough church dates from the 11th century, but its ornately carved rood screen (above) is about 400 years younger, part of the 'spoils' from Henry VIII's dissolution of the monasteries.*

important family and there are several memorials to them in the church. Until the reign of Henry VIII it was customary for the head of the Constable family to stand on Flamborough Head to call to the king of Denmark to collect his dues. When no answer came, he drew his bow and fired a gold coin out to sea.

Although Flamborough **F** has expanded in recent years, the heart of the ancient fishing village remains, with its narrow streets, fishermen's cottages of pale stone with crinkled red roofs, and old pubs. The granite memorial in the centre recalls three Flamborough fishermen swept from *The Two Brothers* and drowned in a great gale in 1909 while trying to rescue the crew of another fishing coble, *The Gleaner,* which had capsized off the headland.

BIRD HAVEN

Bempton Cliffs **G**, among the highest in England, are one of the largest and most important mainland breeding grounds for seabirds. The cliffs are particularly noted for gannet, puffin, razorbill, shag, cormorant, kittiwake and guillemot,

Gannets breed in noisy colonies on rocky stacks and cliffs.

but until relatively recent times the locals regarded their eggs as just another crop. Bempton 'climmers' (climbers) used to work in groups of three, swinging from the ends of ropes in order to reach the nests. As many as 130,000 guillemot eggs were taken every year to be eaten, sold to collectors or sent to Leeds to be used in the patent leather trade. The collecting of eggs was finally outlawed in 1954 and the cliffs now

fishermen. On the south side of the church tower is an effigy of St Oswald and above him some gargoyles. The weather vane, in the form of a fish, reflects the importance of the local fishing industry.

Inside is a Norman font and an unusual stained-glass window shaped like a ship. Near the south door is a pardon from Charles II to Walter Strickland who was ambassador to Holland under Oliver Cromwell. He sailed to America with John Cabot and brought the first turkeys back to England. (A turkey subsequently formed part of his family crest.)

The church's most notable feature is the carved rood screen, thought to have been stolen from Bridlington

Priory after the dissolution of the monasteries. Close examination of the canopied niches reveals traces of red and green paint — all that remains of the images of saints that were removed by the Puritans.

POWERFUL FAMILY

The ruins of a peel tower **E**, built in 1326 by the Constable family of Flamborough, lie in a field. These towers were fortified houses designed to give protection against raiders, particularly the Scots. In the 16th century the building was described as consisting of a tower, hall, great parlour, a lord's parlour, a chapel, courthouse, mill house and great barn. As the size of the building suggests, the Constables were an

form part of a nationally important RSPB reserve, with a clifftop visitor centre at Bempton.

The cliffs around the natural amphitheatre of Thornwick Bay **H** are particularly dramatic: great stacks and arches rising out of the sea like magnificent sculptures. The clifftops are also famous for their wild flowers, which flourish in the chalk grassland. Depending on the time of year, you are likely to see speedwell, pimpernel, orchids, thrift, common fleabane, sea bindweed and poppies.

The large and busy resort of North Landing is the current site of the lifeboat station. All the rescue operations are listed inside, and the treacherous nature of the North Sea unfortunately ensures that the list continues to grow.

Close by is Robin Lythe's cave, 50 feet (15 metres) high inside and one of many similar caves eroded by the sea. It takes its name from a legendary local smuggler whose favourite contraband included brandy, tea and tobacco.

SEA BATTLES

The lighthouse, 85 feet (23 metres) tall, was built in 1805 by John Matson of Bridlington and constructed without scaffolding in only five months. The beam of its 500-watt lightbulb can be seen 21 miles (33.6 km) away. The lighthouse itself is open to the public most afternoons, except Sundays. The foghorn nearby gives two blasts every 90 seconds when visibility is poor — a painful, and frightening, experience if you happen to be passing close by.

About 1/4 mile (400 metres) away, surrounded by a golf course, is the octagonal beacon tower or coal-fired lighthouse built in 1673. In 1959 a toposcope (a stumpy pillar with the compass points and direction of local landmarks indicated on top) was erected near the lighthouse to commemorate the 1779 sea battle between two British men-of-war and four American vessels. The British ships, under the command of Robert Pearson, were entrusted with protecting the Baltic merchant fleet when they were attacked by the

American privateer John Paul Jones. The Baltic fleet escaped, but Pearson, after two hours of fierce sea fighting, was forced to surrender. Even though his flagship, *The Bonhomme Richard*, subsequently sank, Jones has since been honoured with the title 'Father of the United States Navy'.

In the 9th century the headland **L** was invaded by the Danes and many of the rock names have a Danish origin. 'Stacks' derives from 'stakkar', meaning column of rocks, and the blow-hole at Breil Nook gets

◀ *The relentless North Sea has eroded the cliffs of the east coast into mysterious shapes.*

▶ *The octagonal beacon tower, financed by a local entrepreneur, was the first lighthouse on the headland.*

its name from the Danish 'brole', meaning roar. The large, upright rock is called Eve; sadly, Adam has almost eroded away.

Traditional fishing boats

Fishing has long been a mainstay of the Humberside economy, bringing employment to many local families. Although new technology has now infiltrated the industry, not least to pinpoint shoals of fish with greater accuracy, little has changed about the traditional fishing vessel.

The Yorkshire coble is a small, single-masted boat, originally powered by sail and oar, which is based on a design inspired by the Viking longboat. The coble's flat bottom and square stern give it greater stability in the often rough North Sea, but sail power has given way to outboard motors.

At one time donkeys were used to drag the cobles back up the beach after a day's fishing, but tractors now perform this task. Once back on dry land, fish auctions were held on the shore, then hampers of the catch were taken to Flamborough

The coble fishing boat has changed little from the Viking longboat design on which it is based.

station and put on the afternoon train for Hull. Here they would be sold to local shops and restaurants or dispatched to far-flung parts of the country. Tried and trusted over many centuries, the traditional coble is here to stay.

ROUND SPURN POINT

Along sandy beaches rounding the end of a narrow spit of land

Spurn Point lies at the end of a spit of land which reaches out 3½ miles (5.6 km) into the Humber Estuary. About every 250 years, it is cut, washed away and reformed by the tides. The land further north along the coast becomes eroded away and the debris is washed down the coast to come to rest here.

This area is a nature reserve operated by the Yorkshire Wildlife Trust.

FACT FILE

✳ Spurn Point, 12 miles (19 km) south east of Withernsea

⊡ Pathfinder 709 (TA 40/41), grid reference TA 401111

miles 0 1 2 3 4 5 6 7 8 9 10 miles
kms 0 1 2 3 4 5 6 7 8 9 10 11 12 13 14 15 kms

◔ Allow 1 hour

▬ Level walking on the sandy beach. No dogs are allowed on Spurn Point nature reserve

P Charge payable to warden

🍴 Café and inn at Kilnsea on the approach road

WC At the Information Centre

▲ *Spurn Point sits at the end of a long, narrow sand spit. The Arctic skua (right) feeds on the eggs and young of others. It usually hunts alone and intimidates birds bigger than itself.*

It is a popular landing place for migrating birds each spring and autumn and over 32 species of bird have been identified in the area. Among the interesting plants are the small, white-flowered spring beauty and pyramidal orchid. Close to the Information Centre is a Heligoland bird trap used for catching and ringing birds to discover their migration routes. Dunlin have been recovered in France, Sweden and Germany, a meadow pipit in Morocco, blackbirds in Norway and Denmark, plus a starling in Finland.

The car park stands on the site of houses built as military accommodation, once used by the lifeboatmen of the RNLI. Because of its remote situation, the Humber lifeboat is the only one in Britain with a full-time crew. The old lighthouse Ⓐ was built in 1852 and was used at one time as a magazine for storing explosives.

LIFEBOAT HOUSE

The first lifeboat was stationed on Spurn Point in 1810 and, over the years, many lives have been saved and many daring rescues have taken place. The lifeboat house Ⓑ was built in 1923 to accommodate a new Watson-type lifeboat. Coxswain Robert Cross, who operated the lifeboat at this time, was awarded the George Medal, two RNLI gold medals, three silver medals and two bronze medals for gallantry at sea during his 31 years' service.

During summer, part of Spurn Point Ⓒ is fenced off to protect the nesting grounds of the Little Tern. The British population of these birds is just over 2,000 pairs and their nests of two or three eggs are well camouflaged, making it easy for unwary walkers to tread on and destroy them. Behind the beach is an area overrun by sea buckthorn, which offers a haven for migrating birds.

Just offshore lie the Binks Ⓓ, Inner Binks and Middle Binks sandbanks. On a stormy night in 1915 the rowing lifeboat went to the assistance of the SS *Florence*, which had

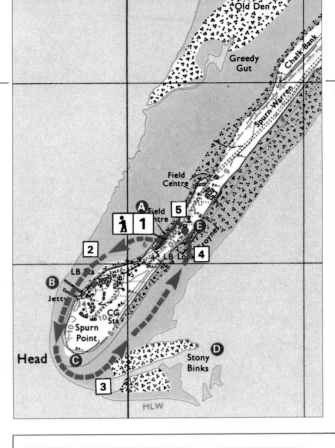

THE WALK

SPURN POINT

The walk begins at Spurn Point car park, 200 yards (180 metres) south of the lighthouse.

1 On your right stands the former lighthouse **A**, surrounded by water. Cross the car park to the concrete wall and descend to the beach by a slipway. This should be possible even at high tide (except during spring tides) and the whole walk is above the high water mark. Turn left towards the jetty.

2 Follow the beach under the Pilots' pier (jetty) and past the old lifeboat house **B**. Continue along the beach to Spurn Point **C** — in early summer, Little Terns breed at this point so avoid passing too close to the colony.

3 Continue around the point and up the coastal side of the site passing the Humber Pilots' control tower on your left. Just offshore are the curious current flows caused by the Binks sandbanks **D**, just below the surface.

4 About 100 yards (90 metres) before you reach the lighthouse **E**, turn left on a path to cross the dunes, passing the circular base of Smeaton's lights, before rejoining the road.

5 Turn left to reach the car park.

run aground on Middle Binks. The lifeboat went aground too, some distance from the ship, so Coxswain Cross walked over the sandbanks taking a line to the ship. In the darkness he was engulfed by waves, but at the second attempt succeeded in getting a line to the ship and rescuing eight seamen. For his courage and bravery he received one of his three RNLI silver medals.

▶ *Currents swirl around the point. Erosion further up the coast forms sandbanks here.*

▼ *The now-disused lighthouse at Spurn Point is visible as far as 17 miles (27 km) away.*

A light was first erected on Spurn Point to guide shipping in 1428. It was looked after by a hermit who took tolls from passing ships. In 1676, another light was built on the point which by then had extended southwards. Trinity House replaced the lighthouse **E** with newer versions in 1771, 1816 and 1831.

RACING CAR

Close to the lighthouse stood the engine sheds of the Spurn Point Railway. The line ran between Kilnsea and Spurn Point and was built during World War 1. As well as regular engines, the line was used by a veteran racing car, converted by an army engineer to fit on the track. There was also a bogie with a sail that operated on the line when there was a favourable breeze.

A WALK ON THE WOLD SIDE

A village, farms and wildlife in Britain's most northerly chalk country

▲The V-shaped sides of Frendal Dale show it was created after the glaciers retreated at the end of the Ice Age. Bloody cranesbill (inset), like other geraniums, grows well on the chalk.

Chalk is the underlying rock of the Yorkshire Wolds, and it has had a great influence on the landscape. Rounded, undulating hills are cut by steep-sided valleys. These were gouged out by melt waters as the ice caps of the last Ice Age retreated. Today, the water table is much lower than the bottom of the valleys, and most of them no longer have any water running in them.

DEEP WATER

The porousness of the chalk has meant that water has always been a precious commodity here. Piped supplies came to the villages only half a century ago. The village of Huggate, which nestles in a fold of the high Wolds, was no exception.

The well on the green **Ⓐ**, where this walk begins, is reputedly the second deepest in the country. According to a sign on a millstone at the site of the well, which is now capped, it is 339 feet (103m) deep. It took two men about half an hour to wind up a single bucket of water, though the water was very pure, having been filtered through hundreds of feet of chalk.

Across the road from the site of the well are some old clay workings **Ⓑ**. A belt of clay runs through the middle of the village, and chalk in the clay lends it a characteristic yellow colour. Bricks baked from the local clay were used in many of the village's more substantial buildings, including Kirkdale House, which was formerly the vicarage.

Downhill from the green is the village pond **C**. In the days of horse power, ponds were vitally important, and every village on the Wolds had one; all the animals drank here, and it also provided water for domestic purposes. The one at

Huggate, dug out of the local clay, is now left mostly to the ducks.

Huggate was once part of a large estate, and has many farm buildings from before the turn of the century. Date stones can still be seen in those constructed by William Jessop,

THE WALK

HUGGATE — FRENDAL DALE

*Begin on the village green **A** at Huggate.*

1 Facing downhill, follow the road past the old clay workings **B** on your right. Pass the village pond **C** and continue round to the left. Turn right into Church Street and continue ahead past St Mary's Church **D** to the sign for Glebe Farm.

2 Turn left along a surfaced farm road, a section of the Wolds Way. Climb steadily. A bridleway takes you past the dewpond **E** with the farm buildings on your right. Continue walking ahead on the farm road.

3 Where it bears left, fork right along a signposted bridleway that runs along a field boundary. At the end, go through the gate and head left along the grassland of Horse Dale. The path bears right into

the bottom of the dale head. Cross the stile and climb steadily, bearing right to the northern corner of the field. Climb over the stile or go through the field gate and walk straight ahead along the field boundary to the road at Huggate Wold Farm. Turn right along the farm track into the farmyard to see the bronze statue of David Midgley **F**.

4 Return along the farm track to a T-junction with a minor road.

5 Turn right. Just before the next road junction, signposted to Thixendale and Fridaythorpe, turn left along a footpath through a hanging wooded valley. At the bottom turn left. The woodland eventually

opens out into hills and pasture. Go through a hand gate and continue along the bottom of Tun Dale, with earthworks **G** visible ahead and to your left-hand side.

6 Bear right along Frendal Dale. Continue through a double gate along the dale bottom, which bears right at first, then left, to a minor road.

7 Cross the road and turn left to follow a grass track parallel to the road. Millington Pasture **H** is on your left.

8 Where the track meets the road, bear right and follow it to a T-junction.

9 Turn left. There may be a view **J** of Hull and the Humber Bridge from this lane. Continue to the crossroads in Huggate and turn left to return to the start.

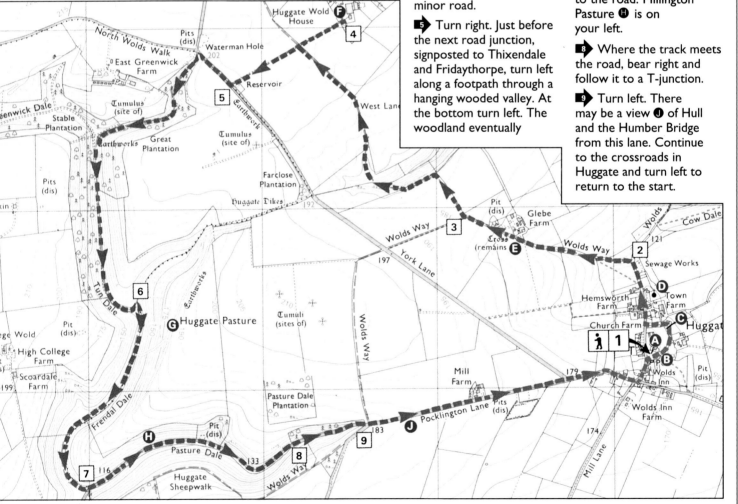

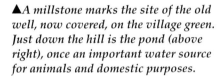

▲*A millstone marks the site of the old well, now covered, on the village green. Just down the hill is the pond (above right), once an important water source for animals and domestic purposes.*

owner of the estate in the late Victorian period, when the village was a thriving farming community.

St Mary's Church ❶, also known as All Saints', is at the north end of the village. It is Norman in origin, but much altered, and its finest feature is the 14th-century tower, surmounted by a splendid spire.

North of the village, you climb steadily along the Wolds Way to the outlying Glebe Farm. As its name suggests, this was once the property of the church. The view from the bridlepath above the farm stretches to the North Sea on the clearest of days, and the light of Flamborough Lighthouse can be seen at night.

DEWPOND

By the route at Glebe Farm , there is a dewpond ❺, an artificial pond that held water for livestock to drink. These ponds were often built in chalk and limestone areas. The oldest of them date back to the 17th century, but pond-makers were still busy until the 1940s.

The manufacture of dewponds was shrouded in mystery. Their builders, known as 'pondies', often added to this by working at night. The ponds are symmetrical hollows

lined with puddled clay. Good ones retain water even in the driest of summers. The pondies' true art was positioning the pond to collect the maximum amount of rainwater running off the land, while allowing as little evaporation as possible. Contrary to what one might expect from their name, they are not designed to gather dew; they are called after their inventor, a Mr Dew.

FINE STATUE

The walk continues through high land planted with cereal crops, mostly barley, and crosses the head

of Horse Dale, a dry valley. At the top of the steady climb, it is worth making a detour along the road to Huggate Wold Farm to see a life-size bronze statue ❻ of David Midgley, a farm foreman, who retired in 1992 after 40 years' service.

◀*The steeple of St Mary's, Huggate, is an important landmark. Less imposing, but more affecting, is the life-size statue of the foreman at Huggate Wold Farm (above).*

▲The route down from the high Wolds into Frendal Dale follows a lovely green way that is an ancient cart-track.

The route continues along a minor road, then down a track into woodland. The walking is easy, and the hanging wooded slopes give you a feeling of stepping back to a time when oxen hauled wooden-wheeled carts up this route.

IRON AGE EARTHWORKS

At the bottom, you walk into the open spaces of Frendal Dale. Above and to the left, along its eastern ridge, earthworks ⦿ are visible. These were made by the Parisii, an Iron Age people thought to have originated in Northern France and to have colonized the Wolds from around 300BC. A local theory is that the ditches and banks were used for coralling and herding livestock.

The end of the dale sweeps round into Millington Pasture ⦿, which until quite recently was open pastureland. Local farmers owned 'gates', not physical barriers but ancient rights to graze a set number of animals in the common pastures. As the route turns east up through the grassland, there is a bounty of wayside flowers. Scabious, knapweed, and bloody and meadow cranesbill make a splendid show in summer, when many butterflies feast on their nectar (see box).

HUMBER BRIDGE

If you look to the right as you climb out of the dale, you may be able to see ⦿ the high-rise flats of Kingston upon Hull, which seem a world away, or the Humber Bridge on the southern horizon. The route goes gently downhill on a country lane towards Huggate, with the distinctive spire of St Mary's Church leading you back to the start.

Wold Wildlife

The Yorkshire Wolds form the most northerly area of chalk in the United Kingdom. The chalky soils have created a specialized habitat in which unique plant and animal communities have evolved.

Before the enclosures of the 17th and 18th centuries, the Wolds were predominantly vast sheep pastures,

The haunting cry of the curlew (left) is often heard from the high ground as you walk along the steep-sided dales (below).

and home to such rare birds as great bustards. Following the enclosures, however, the grasslands were ploughed out for the cultivation of arable crops. Only those areas that were too steep to be planted were left as pasture, and today these are the last refuge of the grassland plants that were once typical of the whole region.

The steep-sided dales are full of wildlife, and many of them are Sites of Special Scientific Interest. Among the important plants are various species of orchid, clustered bellflower, pignut, scabious, harebells and quaking oat-grass, which is common on chalk grassland.

Invertebrates also flourish here, particularly snails and butterflies. In some areas, colonies of the rare marbled white can be found. Common blue, orange tip, small copper ringlet, large skipper and meadow browns are distributed quite widely.

Curlew, grey partridge and whinchat nest here, though suitable breeding sites for all three species are vanishing all the time. The grey partridge, in particular, has been gradually disappearing from our countryside, largely due to intensive arable farming, which destroys its nest sites and insect food.

DOWN ON THE FARM

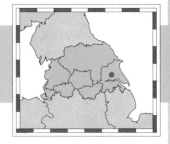

A nature walk in the grounds of an agricultural college

▲ *The horse jumps in the parkland around Bishop Burton are part of a challenging cross-country course. The marsh tit (right), despite its name, is generally found in deciduous woodland.*

Bishop Burton College occupies the estate of what once was the High Hall. Students here study a range of subjects related to the countryside, including wildlife conservation. The college is best known for agriculture, and it includes a large, working farm.

At the start of the Woodland Walk **A** is a vast redwood, planted as a parkland specimen in the days of the High Hall. An information board tells you about the wildlife of the woodland through which you are going to walk. You come to an open glade with a back-cloth of mature yew trees, a marvellous place to spot small birds, particularly in winter, when the thick foliage of the yews provides them with a safe, warm roosting site.

After crossing the playing field, you rejoin the forest trail and the woodland hush returns — unless there is a chainsaw lesson taking place! Along the path, a few steps lift you onto a bank **B** created over 600 years ago, when it had a ditch on either side of it. It is known as The Reins, and was built to keep deer inside the parkland.

The medieval park at Bishop Burton belonged to the Archbishop of York. The earliest reference to it is from 1323, when it was broken into and the deer were stolen. The Reins is by far the most impressive earthwork of its type in the region, and offers you an opportunity to view the floor of the woodland from an unusual height.

GREY TRUNKS

The trees are a mixture of hard and soft woods, some planted recently by students. Other parts have developed into mature high forest, with the magnificent grey trunks of ash trees stretching up into the canopy. In spring, birdsong is everywhere and the sides of the footpath are carpeted with bluebells.

FACT FILE

- ✳ Bishop Burton, 6 miles (9.6km) east of Market Weighton, on the A1079

- Pathfinders 686 (SE 83/93) and 675 (SE 84/94), grid reference SE 986398

  miles 0 1 2 3 4 5 6 7 8 9 10 miles
  kms 0 1 2 3 4 5 6 7 8 9 10 11 12 13 14 15 kms

- ◔ Allow 1½ hours

- ▬ Grassy tracks and well worn trails with a number of stiles

- P Visitors' car park at the start

- The Altisidora pub in Bishop Burton, by the college drive

THE WALK

BISHOP BURTON

The walk begins in the visitors' car park of Bishop Burton College.

1 From the far left-hand corner of the car park, take the signposted route for the Woodland Walk **A**. At the far edge of the woodland, a kissing-gate leads onto the college playing field. Cross the field, to another kissing-gate into the woodland opposite. The path leads onto The Reins **B**. Follow it ahead, and as it bears off to the right.

2 Cross a farm track via two hand gates and rejoin the trail through Oaktree Wood to another hand gate. Go straight ahead towards a field gate that opens out into parkland. The nature reserve **C** is on your right.

3 Enter the park and cross the farm road to a stile on your right. A route parallel to the road crosses a further two stiles. At the second of these, opposite the dairy **D**, go diagonally left across the parkland to another stile onto a road.

4 Cross, climb another stile and walk up through the parkland. Shortly the main college buildings come into view. Bear left to another stile. The visitors' car park, where the walk started, is now in front of you. You can make a detour to take in the walled garden **E** by following the college drive past the main buildings and turning right at the far end of the staff car park.

▲*This lovely walled garden is where students at the college get the chance to show off their horticultural skills.*

The main purpose of the woodland here is to shelter the inner part of the farm from the north-westerly winds that blow down from the Wold tops in winter. At the elbow of the wood, there is a view across part of the college arable land, where groups of students may be receiving instruction. In autumn it is often a busy scene, with sometimes as many as half a dozen tractors working steadily in one field. You will also see some of the jumps that have been constructed for the testing equestrian cross-country course, the venue for an important event in the British Horse Society's calendar. Some of the jumps are huge.

The college nature reserve **C** is tucked away in a section of the woodland, and is well worth exploring if you have the time.

Students have created a woodland pond, and another information board informs you about pond life. Bird and bat boxes have been placed in trees and are numbered to allow students to study their usage.

You emerge from the trees into a very different environment — lovely open parkland. In summer, black and white dairy cattle graze here. A short detour will allow you to visit the college dairy **D**. If you have never watched cows being milked before, time your walk to arrive at the dairy at about 2.45pm.

UDDER INTERESTS

The dairy has been designed so that visitors (and students) can observe milking from a viewing gallery. There is no hustle and bustle here, and the cows queue patiently for their turn. The herdsman and his students milk 120 cows twice a day, every day of the year. Afternoon milking is fairly popular with the students, but the 4.30am duty does not have quite the same appeal!

As you climb up through the parkland trail, the main college buildings come into view on your right. These stand on the site of the old High Hall, which fell into dereliction and was demolished. The new buildings were completed and opened as the East Riding Institute of Agriculture in 1954.

The gardens are kept to a very high standard; the college has a good reputation for horticultural training, something that becomes particularly clear on a visit to the walled garden **E**, which contains many small gardens. These are sure to leave a lasting impression as you return to the visitors' car park.

▼*The route leads along a bank called The Reins, which once had ditches each side and kept the deer in the park.*

ACROSS THE INGS

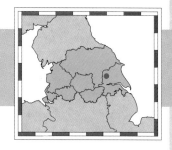

A wildlife walk through a varied lowland landscape

The extensive area of marshes, watermeadows and dykes that makes up the flood-plain of the Yorkshire Derwent provides a number of wildlife habitats. Most of it is protected as the Lower Derwent Valley National Nature Reserve; this walk skirts part of the reserve, at Thornton Ings and Melbourne Ings.

The route starts from the village of Melbourne, and heads for the

FACT FILE

- ✳ Melbourne, 11 miles (17.6km) south-east of York, off the B1228

- Pathfinder 674 (SE 64/74), grid reference SE 753440

  miles 0 1 2 3 4 5 6 7 8 9 10 miles
  kms 0 1 2 3 4 5 6 7 8 9 10 11 12 13 14 15 kms

- ◔ Allow 3 hours

- ▬ Easy walking on canal towpath, level field paths and metalled lanes. Meadowland sections have long, wet grass

- P On the roadside at Melbourne

- The Cross Keys Inn, Melbourne

Pocklington Canal. Opened in 1818, the waterway provides a link between the navigable River Derwent and the market town of Pocklington, at the foot of the Wolds. Although the canal was closed in the 1930s, a considerable length has recently been reopened.

◀ *This hand-operated swingbridge takes a rough track across the canal.*

▲*Bulrushes grow on the banks of the Pocklington Canal near Melbourne. The rich alluvial soil of the flood-plain suits wildflowers such as betony (inset), which is related to hedge woundwort.*

Boats can now travel as far as Melbourne, where a canal basin Ⓐ branches off the main waterway.

East of the basin, the canal's condition immediately begins to worsen; by the time you reach Church Bridge, it is almost silted up. Here you turn onto Church Lane, lined with blackthorn and tall reeds, to approach the village of Thornton Ⓑ, which is a mixture of old agricultural cottages and modern detached houses. Both types are brick-built, and have the pantiled roofs that are characteristic of the East Riding.

WILD FLOWER LANE

At the far side of the village, the route continues along a farm lane. The hedgerows on both sides are thick with wild flowers, and the fields behind them grow a range of crops from maize and wheat to potatoes and sugarbeet. As you turn towards the canal, a view of the escarpment of the Yorkshire Wolds

THE WALK

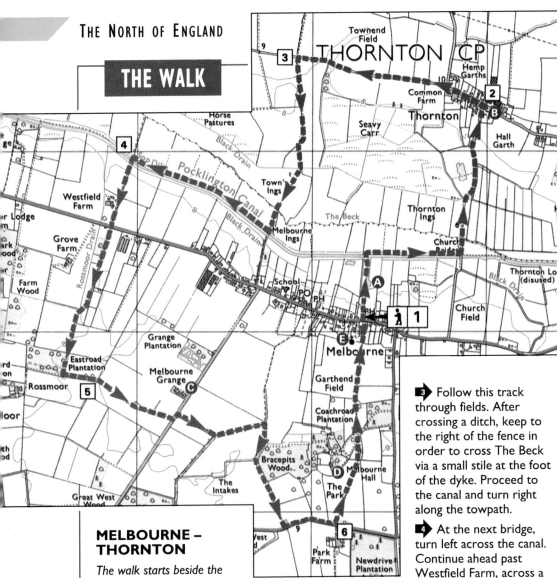

MELBOURNE – THORNTON

The walk starts beside the car park of the Cross Keys Inn at Melbourne.

1 With the pub on your right, walk up the unsurfaced lane, passing the canal moorings **Ⓐ** on your right. Cross the canal bridge and turn right onto the towpath. At Church Bridge, turn left. Follow the lane to Thornton **Ⓑ**.

2 At the T-junction, turn left, through the village. When the road bends right at the cricket pitch, go straight on for about ½ mile (800m). Ignore a broad, grassy track to the left. Some 50 paces further on is a signposted track left.

3 Follow this track through fields. After crossing a ditch, keep to the right of the fence in order to cross The Beck via a small stile at the foot of the dyke. Proceed to the canal and turn right along the towpath.

4 At the next bridge, turn left across the canal. Continue ahead past Westfield Farm, across a road. You pass a farm cottage on your right and a house with a driveway on your left. Keep to the left-hand edge of the field until a waymark points half-right, across to a gap in the hedge. Cross a wooden bridge over a concealed ditch. Follow the left edge of the field and cross a waymarked stile. Go straight ahead into Eastroad Plantation. Take the clearly marked left turn through the shelter belt, and go across the stile into an open field.

5 Cross the field, keeping well right of Melbourne Grange **Ⓒ**, to a stile into a road. Turn left, then right into an attractive green lane. At a junction, keep left and walk along the field edge to the corner. Turn right to follow the near side of the hedge past Bracepits Wood to a road. Turn left.

6 Take the clearly signposted left turn into Melbourne Park, the grounds of Melbourne Hall **Ⓓ**. Head diagonally right towards a gate in the top right corner of the enclosure. Follow the waymarked route ahead up the left edge of the next pasture, to a gate at the end. Turn right onto the driveway. After about 50 paces, cross a waymarked stile to your left. Immediately opposite, across the field, is a second stile. Cross this and follow the field path straight ahead, passing Melbourne's church **Ⓔ** on your left. Pass through a cluster of modern houses and cross the main road to the start.

▼*Horses graze in the mature parkland of 18th-century Melbourne Hall.*

opens up behind you.

You cross Bielby Beck and rejoin the towpath at a swing-bridge. This begins a particularly verdant section of the walk. Mature ash trees line the path, and the lush vegetation supports several kinds of dragonfly. The whole of the canal is designated a Site of Special Scientific Interest for its wildlife value.

South of the waterway, the land changes character, with small copses, and thick hedges dividing the fields. The paths, though waymarked, are often indistinct. Away to your left is Melbourne Grange **Ⓒ**, a substantial brick-built farmhouse.

The route leads round Bracepits Wood. Beyond it is Melbourne Hall **Ⓓ**, a late 18th-century mansion with extensive stables. The approach to it from the road goes through parkland, and the right-of-way passes close to the front of the house.

The final leg of the walk offers views ahead and to the left of Melbourne's church **Ⓔ**. Constructed in 1882, it the most unusual building on the walk; it is roofed, Colonial-style, with sheets of corrugated iron.

LAKELAND BY THE SEA

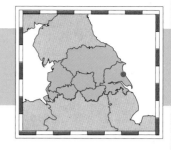

▲*From the site of the medieval village of Southorpe, there is a pleasant view back across the mere to Hornsea. The black tern (left), a scarce visitor, passes through this area on annual migration.*

Discover a wildfowl lake and a Georgian seaside town

Hornsea is an attractive old town with many interesting Georgian buildings, a fine church and an award-winning museum. Its position between the North Sea coast and Yorkshire's largest lake, Hornsea Mere, earned it the title of 'Lakeland by the Sea' in an LNER poster of the 1920s.

The walk starts near the sea front and sets out on the old Hornsea–Hull railway line, which was closed in 1964. The terminus station ❶, in local red brick, has been imaginatively converted into private homes.

Eventually, the embankment descends to a roundabout. On Marlborough Avenue it is worth making a slight detour to Hornsea Pottery ❷ (when open). The site has been developed into a Retail and Leisure Park, and attractions include a butterfly house, a model village, and the Yorkshire Car Collection.

Back on the main route, you

descend through allotments to Hull Road. The route enters meadowland beside Hornsea Mere ❸, an important RSPB Reserve and home to huge numbers of wintering wildfowl and coot.

The route passes the site of the deserted medieval village of Southorpe ❹, one of many in Humberside abandoned during the plagues of the 13th and 14th centuries. Nothing remains of the village apart from some tell-tale undulations at ground level.

AVENUE OF TREES

At the western end of the walk, there is a brief glimpse through the trees to Wassand Hall ❺, a detached Georgian villa in private ownership. Beyond Home Farm, you follow an avenue of magnificent sycamores.

You return round the north side of the mere along field paths, then a surfaced roadside path. Back in Hornsea, the first cottages on Westgate are particularly attractive, and typical of the town's Georgian heritage. St Nicholas' Church ❻, in the town centre, is much older; mainly Perpendicular in style, it was completed between 1400 and 1422 and restored in the mid-Victorian period. The sanctuary is well known for its 'lantern' windows.

Further down Newbegin is the Hornsea Museum ❼. There are local history displays, and many rooms are furnished as they would have been in the late 19th century.

▼*The old station at Hornsea has been tastefully converted for residential use.*

FACT FILE

⁂ Hornsea, 14 miles (22.4km) north-east of Kingston upon Hull, on the B1242

▱ Pathfinders 677 (TA 23/24) and 676 (TA 04/14), grid reference TA 208478

miles 0 1 2 3 4 5 6 7 8 9 10 miles
kms 0 1 2 3 4 5 6 7 8 9 10 11 12 13 14 15 kms

◕ Allow 3 hours

▬ Mostly level walking. Can be muddy around the mere and through fields

P Free car park at the start

▤ Pubs, restaurants and cafés in Hornsea

WC At the start

♖ Hornsea Pottery open 10am–5pm (6pm school holidays) daily. Hornsea Museum open Easter–Oct 10am–5pm

I RSPB reserve information centre at Kirkholme Point, open daily 10am–5pm April–Oct

THE WALK

HORNSEA – HOME FARM

The walk begins in the car park at the bottom of New Road, behind the promenade.

1 Walk away from the sea up Parva Road to the old Hornsea Station **A**. Take the cinder path at the left of the building. Continue along the old track bed. Cross Stream Dike and continue on the embankment, then descend the steep steps to a road and roundabout. Go to the left of the industrial estate, up Marlborough Avenue. At the end, turn sharp right in front of the burial ground gates, where there is a footpath sign.

2 To visit Hornsea Pottery **B**, follow Marlborough Avenue left to a gate in the pottery's perimeter fence. Retrace your steps to the cemetery gates. Ignore the signpost for the railway walk; instead, go straight on, downhill through allotments, to Hull Road.

3 Cross the road and turn left along the pavement. After approximately 200 yards (180m), turn right over a signposted stile, into the meadow beside the mere **C**. Keep to the higher of two paths parallel to the shore, passing the site of the medieval village of Southorpe **D** above to your left. Continue ahead over stiles and through farmland, clipping the southern edge of the marsh called Snipe Ground. Make for the left-hand corner of the wood.

4 Go through the hedge and over a footbridge, and continue to the corner of the next wood. Follow the woodland edge to a gate. A well defined track leads to Home Farm, with Wassand Hall **E** briefly visible away to your left. Beyond the farm, follow the drive down an avenue of sycamores.

5 Just before the end of the avenue, turn left at the waymark, and immediately right through a conifer plantation. Follow the overgrown path between two concrete posts, and out over a stile to a field. Skirt the small pond to pick up a track. Turn right through a white gate, onto Seaton Road. Almost immediately, fork left up Mill Lane and continue for 300 yards (270m).

6 At a footpath sign beneath a tall pylon, turn right over the fields. Follow the waymarks ahead along the field boundaries. Above Buttercup Farm, the path briefly picks up a farm track, then leaves it to pass left of the hedge to another stile. A footpath diversion takes the path left, then along the top of three fields. You emerge on Seaton Road.

7 Turn left, back to Hornsea. At the roundabout, keep right along Market Place, then turn left down Newbegin. You pass the church **F**, then the museum **G**, on your left. Fork right down New Road to Broadway, and the car park.

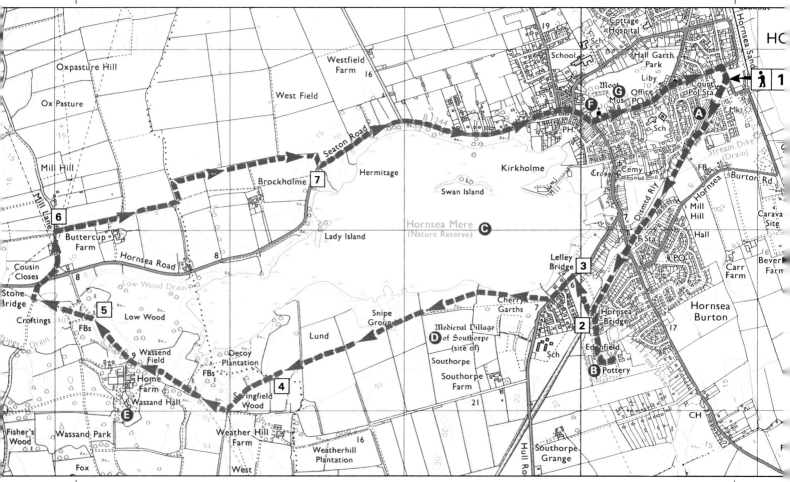

Quiet country lanes in the heart of Lancashire

Once a vast woodland area, the Forest of Bowland today is a forest in name only. The name Bowland comes from the Celtic 'buland', meaning cattle pasture. Cattle still graze across this former hunting ground of Norman kings, which is now steep, bare hills and grassy valleys. Curlews and plovers can be seen flying overhead, and villages nestle around the moorlands, connected by country lanes. The moors and fells of Bowland are popular for walking, bird watching and grouse shooting.

The village of Chipping Ⓐ, where the walk begins, is on the edge of the Forest of Bowland. Its name has had many changes of spelling, and was originally 'Chepyn', from the Old English word meaning market place. It became a market for the surrounding area as far back as Roman times. During the 17th century, Chipping was a prosperous

centre for the wool trade. The sheep were reared on the fells and their wool was used for cloth which was sent to nearby towns, such as Preston. Present-day visitors are attracted by the cobbled pavements and courtyards, the picturesque cottages and almshouses. Most of the village is still laid out to its 17th-century plan, and the main street, Windy Street, is known for its original and beautiful buildings. The corn mill is also standing and is now a restaurant (The Waterwheel).

CHIPPING CHAIRS

Local industry still thrives at Berry & Sons Ⓒ, the Chipping chairmaking firm, which has been in business for over a century. The walk passes through the chair factory grounds, and past Kirk Mill Dam Ⓓ. This head of water provided the power for the works until 1941. The village church, St Bartholomew's Ⓑ, has 'Berry' chairs in the sanctuary, and a stained glass window which

▲ *Kirk Mill Dam provided the power for the chair-making industry in Chipping until 1941. (below) A traditional spindle-backed chair made at the works. (inset) Weasels can be seen in hedgerows and by the roadside.*

FACT FILE

- ✳ Chipping, north-east of Preston, on southern edge of Forest of Bowland

- 🚗 Pathfinder 669 (SD 64/74), grid reference SD 622433

miles 0 1 2 3 4 5 6 7 8 9 10 miles
kms 0 1 2 3 4 5 6 7 8 9 10 11 12 13 14 15 kms

- ◔ Allow 1½ hours

- ▭ Quiet country lanes and farm tracks

- P Off Club Lane, Chipping. Rear of Cobbled Corner Café

- T Bus service from Preston

- WC By car park in Chipping

- 🍴 Cobbled Corner Café, Waterwheel Restaurant, The Talbot Inn (children welcome), The Sun Inn, The Tillotsons Arms, Howden's Homemade Ices

THE WALK

CHIPPING

The walk begins at St Bartholomew's Church **B**, *in the centre of Chipping* **A**.

▶ From St Bartholomew's Church **B** walk up the street which runs between Cobbled Corner Café and the church, passing the car park on the left. Shortly after passing the last of Chipping's houses, leave the main road where it bears left, by walking straight ahead and downhill towards Chipping Chair Factory **C**. The chair factory does not have visitor facilities, but some outdoor activity involving the handling of the raw materials may be seen.

▶ The route through the chair factory is a country lane. Cross the stream and walk up the hill to Kirk Mill Dam **D**. Follow this lane for about 1 mile (1.6 km), passing a new housing development on the left. After climbing another slight hill the lane splits. Keep straight on (the lane is marked as a cul-de-sac) to pass the entrance to

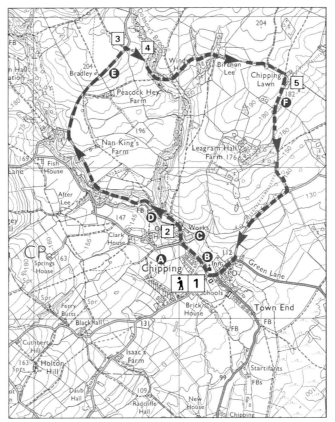

Peacock Hey Farm. The lane gradually climbs uphill, and from the brow of the hill **E**, the views extend towards Longridge Fell (south).

Chipping village is easily recognised by its church tower, nestling in the valley. To the north, the southern slopes of the Forest of

Bowland can be seen.

▶ At the notice 'Unsuitable for Motors', turn right through the gate.

▶ Follow the cart track which passes a house, then go through three gates and a farm where the track becomes a concrete drive. Cross two cattle grids to arrive at a second farm, Chipping Lawn Farm (also called Laund Farm).

▶ Bear right to reach an excellent viewpoint **F**. To the south, the view extends across the Loud and Ribble valleys with Longridge Fell in the middle distance, and further on to the south-east is Pendle Hill — also known as the 'Witches Hill' — rising 1327 feet (540 metres) above the Ribble. Follow the concrete drive for another ¹/₂ mile (800 metres), twisting gently downhill to a country lane for Chipping and at the T-junction turn right for the centre of the village to return to the church and the start of the walk.

commemorates the life and work of John Berry, who died in 1966.

Once beyond the village, at points **E** and **F** on the map, there are magnificent views. From this height, the atmosphere and spirit of this uncluttered landscape can be appreciated in full. The fells, Longridge, Parlick, Wolf and Saddle stretch into the distance, and the skyline of Chipping can be seen in the valley. Another striking landmark, Pendle Hill, is also known as the 'Witches Hill' after the witches of Pendle tried for sorcery in 1612.

▲ *St Bartholomew's Church contains a modern memorial window to John Berry, while the font dates from 1520.*
▶ *Chipping's Windy Street still has many of its 17th-century houses.*

Longridge Fell on the skyline, viewed from Chipping Lawn Farm.

THE FOREST OF BOWLAND

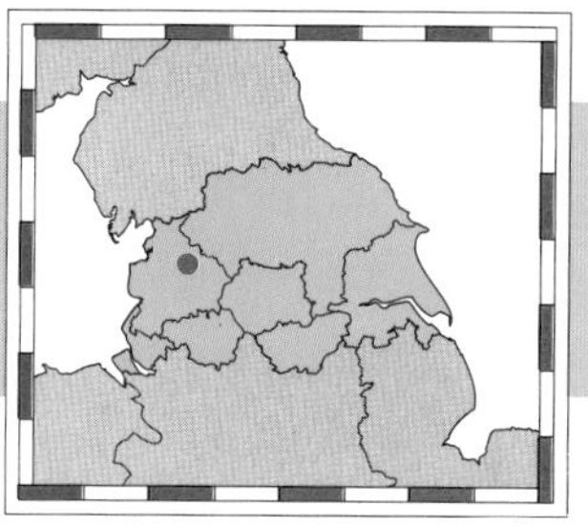

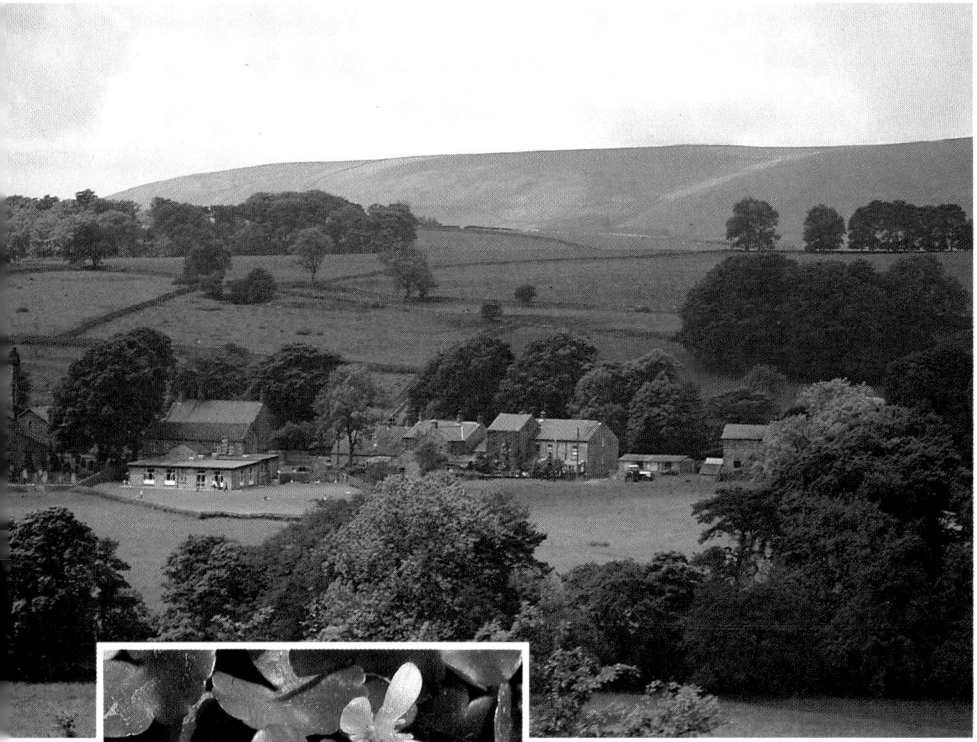

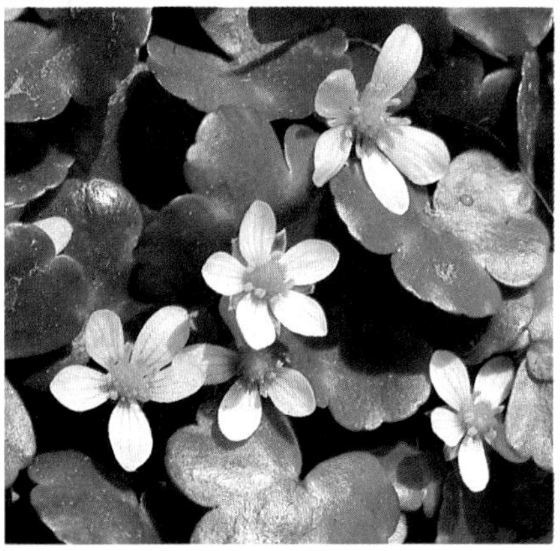

▲*The village of Slaidburn has a fine Gothic church, rebuilt during the reign of Henry VI. Ivy-leaved water crowfoot (left) grows in ponds and ditches as well as in slow-moving streams.*

A forest of Royal hunts and a million oaks

The Forest of Bowland is a plateau of heather-clad hills and moors, cut by deep, green valleys. The word 'forest' derives from the old English *foris* — land devoted to the royal sport of hunting. Red and fallow deer, as well as wild boar, were hunted by Anglo-Saxon kings and Norman barons.

Henry VI used the isolation of Bowland to his advantage — after his defeat at Hexham, he hid here for a year, before being betrayed and ambushed while crossing the River Ribble by stepping stones.

This century, sika deer, an Asiatic species, were introduced to Bowland by Lord Ribblesdale. Roe deer, a native of Britain, can also be spotted around here. The first Lord Ribblesdale, Thomas Lister, lived from 1752-1826. He made his contribution to the area by planting over a million oaks and other trees.

At the start of the walk, there is an inviting grassy bank on the riverside opposite the car park. In the nineteenth century, hundreds of rabbit skins were pegged out here and used to make beaver-style hats.

BURNING BRACKEN

The names of the fells are a reminder of the past. Salter Fell was on the route of a packhorse trail used to bring salt to the outlying farms for preserving meat. Rising from Slaidburn itself is Tenter Hill **A**. Here, locally made rolls of woollen cloth were hung from tenterhooks for a softening treatment with potash, which was made by burning bracken. Near Tenter Hill is the rolling farmland and woodland of the area known as Woodhouse **B**. In the 14th century, the Abbot of Kirkstall Abbey, near Leeds, owned a great deal of land in Bowland, and Woodhouse was then used as a stud for the Abbot's horses.

GOLDEN PLOVER

In late summer, the moorland view is coloured with purple, cross-leaved heath and orange bracken. As well as moorland birds — lapwing, curlew and golden plover — there are thousands of black-headed gulls. They breed on an island in Stocks Reservoir, just out of sight beyond Woodhouse. The island is also home to nesting geese, as well as red-breasted merganser and wintering goosander.

Field paths lead to Easington **C**, an old settlement mentioned in the Domesday book. The site of the old manor house has been excavated, revealing walls over 4 feet (1.2 metres) thick. The path from Easington returns you to a tranquil section of the River Hodder **D**. These quiet reaches are ideal for spotting birds such as sandmartins, sandpipers, dippers, heron, oystercatchers and redshank.

FACT FILE

- Slaidburn, 7 miles (11 km) north of Clitheroe
- Pathfinder 660 (SD 65/75), grid reference SD714523
- miles 0 1 2 3 4 5 6 7 8 9 10 miles / kms 0 1 2 3 4 5 6 7 8 9 10 11 12 13 14 15 kms
- Allow about 2 hours
- Rough fields; grassy or stony tracks, tarmac lanes. Parts of the route could be muddy at times
- Drinks, lunches and high teas at the Hark to Bounty Inn. River Bank snack bar sells home-made cakes, tea, coffee, ice cream etc
- WC By the car park

THE WALK

SLAIDBURN – EASINGTON

The walk starts from the car park at Slaidburn.

1 Leave the car park, and cross the road to the river bank. Turn left and cross the bridge over the River Hodder. Walk uphill out of the village. After about 300 yards (270 metres), the road makes a sharp left turn.

2 Shortly after the turn, go through the wide wooden gate on the right. From here there are good views over Slaidburn and the surrounding fellside, including Tenter Hill **A** and Woodhouse **B**. Bear half right, uphill, following the faint track across the grass towards the trees seen on the right. When you reach the boundary wall continue along the field, keeping the wall on your right.

3 About 30 yards (27 metres) before you reach the corner of the field, there is a metal gate in the wall, set between two large slabs of rock. Next to the gate there is a rough stone stile in the wall. Cross this and continue along the next field, parallel to its boundary wall on your left.

4 Immediately after passing a little wood on the left, there is a metal gate in the wall. Cross through and continue in the same direction as before, going downhill, and with the wall now on your right.

5 At the bottom of the slope, cross a little wooden stile over a wire fence to join a tarmac lane. Turn right and then walk along the lane as far as the

hamlet of Easington **C**. Shortly after passing through Easington, the road runs parallel to a beck on the left, then bends to the right.

6 On the bend, through a metal gate, there is a track leading away to the right. Follow this track between the fences to the end, where the path opens out into a field. Turn right, passing another metal gateway, onto a grassy track. The track passes through a wooden gate between a belt of trees. Carry on along the field with a wire fence to your left. The track leads towards the River Hodder **D**. Dunnow Hall **E** can be seen ahead, to the left.

7 Cross the river by a little bridge with parapets. Continue along the track, which passes close to Dunnow Hall then veers right, skirting the edge of woods.

8 Cross a wooden stile and join the road, turning right to enter the village past the church **F** and school **G**. At the end of the road, opposite the Hark to Bounty Inn **H**, a right turn soon brings you back to the starting point.

A little bridge crosses the river and bears right, past Dunnow Hall **E**. The Hall was built in the 1830s for the Wilkinsons, but the family never lived there. Tragically, while the first owner and his wife were honeymooning in Switzerland, the coach in which they were travelling slipped over the cliff edge of an Alpine track. Mr Wilkinson survived, but his new bride was killed.

A quiet lane leads back towards the village. The first building you reach is the church **F**, whose history can be traced back over eight centuries. Near the church, traces of a Bronze Age settlement have been

discovered and next to it is the old Grammar School **G**, founded in 1717. It is of an unusual English architectural style — the Carolean.

At the far end of the lane is the Youth Hostel, previously the Bull Inn. Opposite the hostel is the Hark to Bounty Inn **H**. The story goes that it changed its name from the Dog Inn in 1875, after a hunt when the Reverend Henry Wigglesworth picked out the sound of his hound, Bounty, from all the others baying outside the inn. The upstairs of the Hark to Bounty contains all the original furnishings from the time when it was the local courthouse.

▼*The course of the River Hodder was changed slightly when a reservoir was built over the ruins of Dalehead village.*

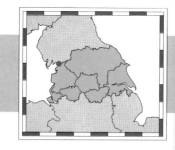

Through rugged coastal countryside to an historic country seat

▲*At Jack Scout, the limestone crag juts out into Morecambe Bay. The brown aeshna (inset) is a hawker dragonfly and patrols its waterside territory.*

The walk visits Lancashire's impressive coastal limestone crags in the far north-west of the county. Much of the area is designated an Area of Outstanding Natural Beauty, while the other areas are protected as nature reserves. There are rare birds, plants, animals and butterflies as well as coastal flats, immense views over the Lake District and a flamboyant Gothic mansion — and all of them in a quiet corner of England where you can enjoy peace and solitude even at the height of summer.

Warton itself is an ideal place to start. This ancient village has a few winding back streets and ginnels (alleys) lined with tiny cottages. There are also some yeomen's houses built of the native limestone. The village seems to sprout quite naturally from the foot of the crag that bears its name.

At the south end of the oldest part of Warton is St Oswald's Church Ⓐ which dates, in part, from the 13th century. The present tower was added 200 years later. It was largely paid for by a local benefactor, Robert Washington — his old family house is opposite the post office. He incorporated the family coat of arms into the design of the building. In 1789 one of his descendants, George Washington, became the first President of the United

FACT FILE

☀ Warton, 2 miles (3.2 km) north of Carnforth

🗺 Pathfinder 636 (SD 37/47), grid reference SD 497724

miles 0 1 2 3 4 5 6 7 8 9 10 miles
kms 0 1 2 3 4 5 6 7 8 9 10 11 12 13 14 15 kms

◔ Allow 4½ hours

▬ Some steep climbs and some slippery sections, so unsuitable for small children. Minor roads, fields, woodland and sea marsh

🅿 In Warton at the small car park 50 yards (46 metres) up Crag Road, the turning beside The Black Bull

🚆 Regular bus services run daily between Warton and Lancaster via Carnforth. By rail you can pick up route of walk at Silverdale station (in Stage 6)

🏪 Shops and three pubs in Warton, café at Leighton Moss Visitor Centre

🏰 Leighton Hall, open afternoons May to September

ℹ Conducted walks around nature reserve available, commencing from Leighton Moss Visitor Centre, Tel. (01524) 701601

THE WALK

WARTON – SILVERDALE GREEN

The walk starts in the small car park in Warton, just behind The Black Bull Inn on Crag Road.

1 Walk up the narrow path from the back of the car park. Turn right at the top beside the information board, then left 20 yards (18 metres) later. Walk gradually uphill along this natural step in the limestone crag (with the spire of St Oswald's Church **A** behind and to your left) to the fence at the top. Cross the stile and walk ahead for about 30 yards (27 metres), with an old quarry to your left. Take the obvious path, right, some distance your side of the perched boulders. Cross the area of plateau, climbing up onto the next 'step'. Aim for the low cliff face at the far side (virtually straight ahead), climb the high wooden stile beneath the ash trees and work your way up to the summit of the Crag **B**.

2 With the trig point and the beacon pole on your right, walk away from the summit. Follow the signposted path towards Crag Foot. Wind through the predominantly ash woodland, following occasional signs. On reaching the rough, walled tractor path, Occupation Road, turn left and continue for about ½ mile (800 metres) until you reach a minor road. Turn right down this and walk to the junction. Go straight ahead, then bear left with the road out across the Mossland.

3 At the sharp bend bear left and follow the rough road beneath the railway, then turn right and cross the stone bridge across the drain. Climb the gate and turn left, climbing a further stile before curving left with the embankment. Climb a further stile and bear right with the embankment, following it across the sea marsh. At the far end turn left, following the sign to Jenny Brown's Point, shortly passing by an isolated chimney stack **C**. Remain with the shoreline to reach the cottages known as Brown's Houses.

4 Join the narrow tarmacked road just beyond the cottages and follow this along the low cliff. Go through the kissing gate on the left to gain access to Jenny Brown's Point **D** and Jack Scout. Stick to the (indistinct) coastal path to end up high above a sandy inlet. Regain the road by following the fence/wall away from the coast and through the trees to reach the roadside wall. Look for the exit gate and turn left, passing by Lindeth Tower **E** on your left. Turn right along Hollins Lane, pass the craft centre and walk along to the band of trees. Turn left at the sign to Woodwell, favouring the path along the top of the ridge and beside the meadow. Bear gradually left through the trees and climb the stile into the long, narrow pasture. Bear right to the signpost on the bank and left here towards The Green, funnelling in to the narrow meadow end.

5 Climb the stile at the end of the glade and follow the line of wall on your right. At the green door, turn right along the walled/ fenced path and continue beyond along the driveway to the road. Turn right along this to Silverdale Green. Turn left along Bottoms Lane towards Arnside and Milnthorpe. Just past the last house on the right, take the signposted path on the right to Burton Well. Near the well climb the stile out of the woods and walk along to the footbridge. Cross this and walk across to the ladder stile. Climb this and turn left, following the path up the steps and through the woods. Go straight ahead at the crossing of paths and alongside the garage to the road.

6 Turn right and 50 yards (46 metres) later go left at the worn footpath sign and onto the golf course. Pass to the left of the two bare mounds but to the right of the one with fir trees. On gaining the road, turn right and walk along past Silverdale station. Turn left

▲*The steep ascent up Warton Crag leads you over ridges and hollows worn into the limestone by rain-water.*

States. The Stars and Stripes flag adopted by that new country is based on the heraldic designs of the Washington coat of arms. Another very famous statesman, Winston Churchill, also has connections by marriage with Warton. Details of both these men's family trees are displayed in the church. Just down-hill from St Oswald's are the remains of a 14th-century rectory.

AN OLD BRITISH FORT

From the village, it is a fairly steep walk up Warton Crag **B**, the reward being the enormous views that open up across Morecambe Bay, while behind you are the austere heights of the Forest of Bowland. Once you reach the summit of the Crag, a grand panorama of the mountains of southern Lakeland forms the horizon. This peak is the site of an old British fort, although evidence is obvious only to those who know what to look for. It has also seen use as the site of a beacon at the time of, for example, the Spanish Armada and the threatened invasion during the Napoleonic Wars. To the south, the large concrete buildings are Heysham Nuclear Power Station. In the distance beyond these is Blackpool's famous Tower.

The Crag itself is a nature reserve renowned for its variety of butter-flies — including the high brown fritillary and the (anything but) common blue, for example. The rare, lime-loving plants found on its slopes, as well as in its ridges and hollows, are diagnostic features of

across the railway bridge to reach the Visitor Centre at Leighton Moss **F**. Continue along the road and start to walk uphill. Immediately past the cottage (set back from the road and behind a hedge) on the right, go down the track and out across the Moss. Climb the gate at the far end and follow the track to Grisedale Farm. Remain with the roadway from here to reach Leighton Hall **G**.

7 Follow the drive away from the Hall and bear left, following the line of telegraph poles very steeply up across the parkland. At the ridgetop, turn right and walk along to the woodland. Climb the stile behind the green wooden fencing and walk through the woods to the minor road. Turn right along this and walk the remaining 1 mile (1.6 km) back to Warton. Turn right in the village to return to the car park where the walk began.

limestone country. The ridges are called clints and the fissures between them grikes. They were made by slightly acidic rainwater dissolving away limestone along pre-existing cracks over tens of thousands of years. In parts of Cumbria, and even more so in the Yorkshire Dales, there are vast areas of such features, which are referred to as limestone pavements.

CRAG FOOT

Warton Crag is an outlier of the mountain limestone which forms much of the Dales. The natural steps in the steep southern face were formed about 300 million years ago during the geological Carboniferous period. As you walk through the woods on the way to Crag Foot,

◀*Jenny Brown's Point, where a chimney stands by the marsh, is named after an old lady who lived in nearby cottages.*

look out for red squirrels and listen for the 'shee-shee' call of the gold-crest, Britain's second smallest bird. You may also catch a fleeting glimpse of a stoat or a weasel scurrying across Occupation Road.

On either side of the low-lying marshy mossland, isolated old chimneys **C** can be seen. These are evidence of the copper smelting industry that flourished in the area two centuries ago. Coniston was, at this time, the major centre, ore being carried by mule, cart, boat and rail to small ports such as Greenodd (just to the west of Warton) for export. Smaller deposits were worked in many parts of the Lake District. These smelting works used the local limestone as a flux to balance chemical reactions when the ore-bearing rock was heated in order to release the metal.

MARSHES AND MUDFLATS

The walk along the edge of the marsh affords extensive views of this corner of Morecambe Bay — eerie marshes and mudflats dotted with old fence posts, ever changing river channels and areas of quicksand. It is a favourite feeding ground for oystercatcher, redshank, knot, curlew and heron. Look out, too, for little owls. During the summer months, steam-hauled rail excursions ply along the marsh on their way from Carnforth to

Sellafield. The Flying Scotsman can sometimes be seen (Tel. [01524] 732100).

As the walk progresses around Jenny Brown's Point **D**, the mountains of the southern Lake District once again come to dominate the horizon. At the Point and neighbouring Jack Scout, a low headland of limestone juts out into the marshlands, quicksands and sandbanks. This is a bountiful feeding ground for myriad wading birds, ducks and gulls. Both are under the protection of the National Trust. Further on, Lindeth Tower **E** (also known as

Leighton Moss Nature Reserve

Leighton Moss is owned by the RSPB, the reserve being primarily established to conserve the habitat of the rare bittern, whose ethereal booming call you may hear echoing across the marshes. It is a huge area of ponds, ditches and meres at the head of a great sea marsh.

By more than a happy coincidence, countless other rare and endangered wildfowl also make a home here — bearded tit, scaup, gargeney and eider for example. Ospreys are occasional visitors and it is one of the few places to see marsh harriers. The waters and woodlands are also home to otters, red squirrels, red, fallow and roe deer. The Moss has been in the natural state you see today since

The nature reserve at Leighton Moss is situated in a huge expanse of sea marsh. The heron is one of many birds seen here.

1917 — before this the whole area was rich farmland, artificially kept free of water by a complicated system of ditches and pumps.

There is a fine visitor centre at Myers Farm, which the RSPB purchased to enable the establishment of the reserve in 1964. Permits to enter the reserve may be obtained here (you do not need a permit to follow this walk and there is a public hide on the route). The comedian Eric Morecambe was an enthusiastic supporter of the reserve and one of its pools is named after him.

◀*The halfway point of the walk is at Silverdale Green. It is possible to start the walk from the station here. Further along the route, near Leighton Hall, is beautiful woodland scenery (right).*

Gibraltar Tower) is an eccentric folly, but one that can be lived in. A resident in years gone by was the novelist Mrs Gaskell (1810-65) who partly based one of her novels, *Ruth*, on that area; Charlotte Brontë is said to have visited her here.

After the scattered community of Silverdale Green you come to the flat expanse of the nature reserve at Leighton Moss **F**. The embankment across the Moss, protected from the worst of any storms by some high stands of reeds, leads to the estate road to Leighton Hall **G**.

HISTORIC HORNBY

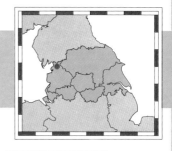

FACT FILE

- Hornby, 9 miles (14km) north-east of Lancaster

- Pathfinders 637 (SD 56/57) and 650 (SD 66/76), grid reference SD 585683

  miles 0 1 2 3 4 5 6 7 8 9 10 miles
  kms 0 1 2 3 4 5 6 7 8 9 10 11 12 13 14 15 kms

- Allow 3½ hours

- Tarmac lanes, a track and fields; long grass may be wet

- P Free car park behind the bridge in Main Street

- T Buses from Lancaster, Settle and Kirkby Lonsdale. Tel. (01524) 841656 for details

- Hornby: shops and tea room; Royal Oak serves bar meals; Castle Hotel. Wray: George and Dragon Inn serves coffee and meals

◄ *There has been a castle at Hornby for around 900 years and it has passed through many hands. The present building is largely Victorian. Honeysuckle (inset) bedecks the hedges locally. The Cat and Rat Keystone (below) is a reminder of the railway.*

From two castles to a village where industry once thrived

There are many glimpses of the past on this walk around the villages of Hornby and Wray, in Lancashire's Lune valley. The starting point is the bridge over the River Wenning, built in 1769, which carries the main road through Hornby.

Historians think that Hornby was once the site of a villa belonging to a wealthy Roman. The evidence is the discovery of Roman coins and a brick pavement, and its proximity to Lancaster and the Roman camp at Barrow-in-Furness.

During the Norman Conquest, Hornby was in the hands of Alric, a Saxon chieftain. Later, it passed by marriage to de Montbegon, who came over from France with William's conquering army. The foundations of Hornby Castle **A** were probably laid by Montbegon, on the site of the Roman villa. After Montbegon, the castle was owned by the deBurghs, followed by the de Nevilles, then the Harringtons.

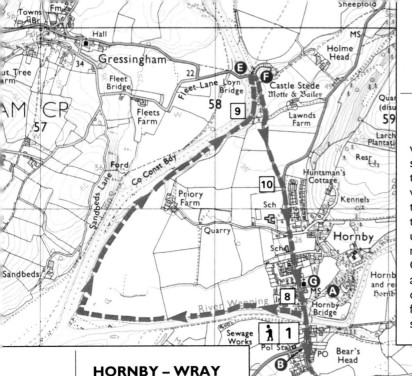

woods, using the stone-step stile. Walk along the edge of the woods, and cross two wooden stiles close together. Pass to the left of the next gate, and walk uphill to pass through a metal gate into a field. Cross the field, go through another metal gate, and continue downhill, with the fence on your right, and the stream down below to the

crossing a stone-step stile, then a wooden stile. At the confluence of the two rivers, turn right, to follow the bank of the River Lune.

9 As you near Loyn Bridge **E**, cross a wooden ladder stile into the woods. Follow the woodland path, then cross another ladder stile to reach the river edge. Pass under the arch of the bridge, then turn right, up

HORNBY – WRAY

The walk starts from the car park behind Hornby Bridge.

1 Turn right, to walk south through Hornby. Hornby Castle **A** can be seen across the river. Where the main road bears right, towards Lancaster, take the minor road straight ahead (Station Road). The Cat and Rat Keystone **B** is located at this junction.

2 At the crossroads, turn left and walk up the lane for a short distance.

3 Just before the road sign for Wray, take the track on the left. This is Back Lane.

4 When you reach a crossroads of tracks, turn right, towards houses. At the road, turn left, and walk past the Methodist church on the right, and Duck Street on the left. At the road junction, turn right, past the George and Dragon, into the main

street of Wray **C**.

5 Just before the post office and shop, take a right turn, signposted 'Roeburndale West'. Go uphill for a short distance.

6 At a public footpath sign, take the field path on the right, next to a wooden bench and field gate. Walk through the field, keeping the wall on your right. When you draw level with the woods on the right, cross the wall towards the

left. Cross a wooden stile in the fence ahead to join Moor Lane.

7 Turn right along the lane, soon passing the stone cross **D**. At the crossroads, go straight on. Cross the old railway bridge and return to Hornby Bridge. Cross it and go through the wooden gate on the left, following a public footpath sign on the wall.

8 The path runs alongside the River Wenning, first

the river bank, to rejoin the road. Turn left, and in about 50 yards (45m) look for a public footpath signpost on the left, indicating a narrow gap in the wall which gives access to the motte and bailey **F**. Rejoin the road, turning left towards Hornby.

10 At the road junction, follow the main road into Hornby, passing St Margaret's Church **G** on the left, just before reaching Hornby Bridge.

Later, the castle was inherited by the Stanley family. Sir Edward Stanley fought at the Battle of Flodden (1513), supported by local yeomen. Sir Edward restored the 13th-century keep, which is the oldest surviving part of the castle. He also built the octagonal tower (1514) at the Parish Church of St Margaret, as a thanksgiving for victory.

During the Civil War, the castle was owned by the Parkers, and was a Royalist stronghold. After it was captured, Cromwell ordered it to be destroyed. Fortunately, this was never done, and a succession of later owners have each extended and improved the castle. The present castle is mostly 19th-century.

The atmospheric setting of the

castle, with its keep, turrets, battlements and mullioned windows, set high on a mound above the River Wenning, was appreciated by artists and poets. Three of Turner's best-known drawings are of Hornby Castle, or the view from it. Thomas Grey wrote about the valley of the Lune and of the lands that were once part of Hornby Castle estates.

Hornby's situation between two fordable rivers, the Wenning and the Lune, means that a road has always passed through the village, making Hornby a centre of Lune valley life.

DAWSON'S STONE

The railway arrived later. At the end of the main street, you pass an unusual stone built into a wall above the fountain, depicting a cat holding a rat in its mouth. The monogram 'PD' on the stone stands for Pudsey Dawson, one of the originators of the railway line that ran from Wennington to Morecambe. The Cat and Rat Keystone ❸ was re-sited here when one of the stone railway bridges was replaced by a wider iron bridge.

On the next part of the walk, a bridge crosses the old railway, then lanes and tracks lead to Wray ❸, situated where the River Roeburn meets the River Hindburn. Wray is a village settled by Norsemen, 'wray' meaning 'an out of the way corner'. The main street has cobbled pavements, with 17th-century farms,

▲*Though nestled in an agricultural landscape, the village of Wray was once a busy centre of industry. The arches of the medieval Loyn Bridge (below) cross the River Lune north of Hornby.*

barns and cottages lining the road. Many of the cottages, set about with pretty gardens and window boxes, have datestones on their lintels.

SILK AND CLOGS

In Wray, farming and industry developed side by side. In years past, this quiet place was a hive of industry. There was a mill along the bank of the Roeburn, employing 100 people to spin the raw silk that came into the Lune docks from China; it was then turned into silk hats. In the village, there were woodturners, nail makers, bobbin makers, wheelwrights and clog blockmakers.

The hedgerows of blackthorn, hawthorn and cherry, which line the lane on the way back towards Hornby, are interlaced with dog rose, downy rose and guelder rose, intertwined with honeysuckle and bindweed. The banks and verges support wood violets, primroses, dog's mercury, cuckoo pint, celandine and stitchwort, as well as stands of garlic mustard and cow parsley. Meadow cranesbill and greater bellflower may also be spotted. The hedgerows are popular in winter with fieldfares, redwings and other thrushes.

On the verge is a well-preserved stone cross ❶, a waymark on the old north-south packhorse trail, which went south across the fells above Wray. The packhorses carried salt and other vital goods. In the field behind the cross, the depression marks the old route. Nearing Hornby, at Butt Yeats, you pass the massive base of another stone cross.

▼*This weathered stone cross by the lane on the return to Hornby was a waymark on the old packhorse trail.*

The next part of the walk is along the river banks of the Wenning and the Lune. There are several kinds of willow to be found on the river banks, and these were used in the past by the basket-makers of Arkholme, to the north of Hornby.

At the river's edge, there are areas of sand and shingle, where dippers and wagtails are often seen and waders such as oystercatchers and common sandpipers search for food. The sandy banks provide nesting sites for sand martins. In winter, greylag geese fly over in formation to their feeding grounds.

ONE OF A KIND

Where the rivers meet, a priory existed 800 years ago. There is no trace of it now, but in the Parish Church of St Margaret in Hornby, below the octagonal tower, there are fragments of two crosses from the priory. One of these was chiselled over 1,000 years ago, and depicts the Bible story of the Loaves and Fishes. This cross is unique in England. There are also tomb lids from the priory, with carvings of swords and chalices. A look at the churchyard also reveals the base of an Anglo-Saxon cross.

MASONIC SECRETS

You leave the river bank at Loyn Bridge ❺, which carries the road across the Lune to Gressingham. It is a medieval stone bridge, bearing many masons' marks. The masons were required to put their own

▼ *St Margaret's Church, with its octagonal tower, contains artefacts from the now defunct priory.*

Motte and Bailey Castles

The grassed-over earthworks that are found around the bailey at Castle Stede were originally thrown up by the Normans.

When the Normans conquered Britain in 1066, they brought with them a new style of fortification, the motte and bailey castle. The motte was a conical mound of earth, on top of which was built a defensive tower, or keep. The bailey was an outer enclosure at a lower level, defended by a wall. The motte and bailey were joined by a drawbridge, and the whole structure was surrounded by a ditch.

The keep was sometimes built of stone, and was often incorporated into a larger castle at a later date, but it was more usual for the buildings to be made of timber. Living quarters, stables and granaries were in the bailey.

Sometimes the motte was produced by steepening the sides of a natural hill. When the motte was made by artificial means, it was more than a simple mound of earth, which would have been unstable. It was composed of alternate layers of stone and beaten earth.

Often, the motte was coated with a thick layer of clay, which prevented erosion and made it harder for attackers to scale the slope. Some mottes were of modest size, maybe only 20 feet (6m) high. At the other end of the scale, there are mottes with summits up to 100 yards (90m) in diameter.

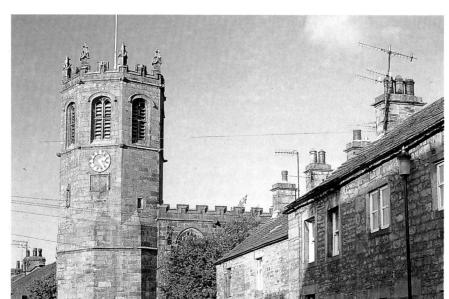

individual mark on their stones, so that their workmanship could be checked by the master mason. Each gang or 'lodge' had its own secret signs to prevent the entry of unskilled workers.

Above Loyn Bridge is a fine example of a Norman motte and bailey ❻. Called Castle Stede, the site covers about 2¹/₂ acres (6 hectares), and both sections have moats. The pudding-shaped motte is overgrown with trees, and there are raised earthen defences around the level bailey. From here, the lane soon brings you back past St Margaret's Church ❼ into Hornby.

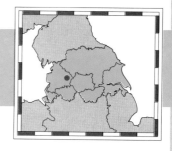
LANCASHIRE

A walk up Pendle Hill and over Lancashire's moorlands

The whaleback hump of Pendle Hill stands alone, dominating the plains surrounding Burnley, Nelson and Colne. Its distinctive profile can be viewed from Yorkshire, Lancashire and Cumbria.

The walk starts at the village of Barley Ⓐ. Back in 1324 it was known as Barelegh, meaning the infertile lea, or meadow. The area depended on agriculture until the early 18th century when the textile industry developed. It became normal to install a hand loom in the home, as an extra source of income. There was also a cotton mill in Barley, with 200 looms, but in the 1880s a flood destroyed the business. Ironically,

the building is now owned by the North West Water Authority.

Pendle is a plateau of high, airy moors, covering an area of 20 square miles (52 square km). To the north and east are steep escarpments, and there are several cloughs — narrow valleys or ravines — that cut into the moor. Ogden Clough provides the water catchment for the Ogden reservoirs, which you can see to the south from the top of Pendle Hill Ⓑ.

FIRE-BEACON

The 1,827-foot (557-m) summit is marked by a triangulation point at the mount known as Big End, or the Beacon. This refers to a fire-beacon, which was used to signal a warning or news of any important events. A look-out was posted at the Beacon, to watch for approaching bad weather at haymaking time. Nowadays, walkers can appreciate

◄ *Where the path leads from Ing Ends towards Brown House, Pendle Hill dominates the way ahead. The hen harrier (below left) is scarce but may be seen hunting over Pendle's moorlands.*

FACT FILE

✳ Barley, 5 miles (8km) north of Burnley

🗺 Pathfinder 670 (SD 84/94), grid reference SD 823403

miles 0 1 2 3 4 5 6 7 8 9 10 miles
kms 0 1 2 3 4 5 6 7 8 9 10 11 12 13 14 15 kms

🕐 Allow 3 hours

▬ Paths can be muddy. A steep ascent and a stony path on the descent

🅿 Free car park in Barley

🍴 Snack bar in car park. Tea shop, Pendle Inn and Barley Mow pub all in Barley

🚾 In car park (including disabled access)

ℹ Information Centre in Barley car park, open daily Apr-Oct: weekends Nov-Mar; Tel. (01282) 601893

THE WALK

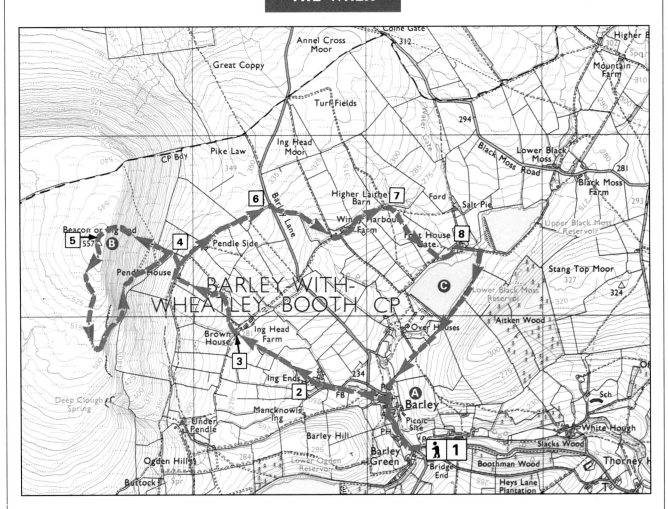

BARLEY – PENDLE HILL

The walk begins in Barley Ⓐ, in the car park and picnic area by the stream.

1 Turn right out of the car park, then right again through the village. Just before the post office, take the path on the left, alongside a stream. Follow this path, soon crossing a stile. A little further on, cross the bridge over the stream on the right. Turn left and walk along the tarmac lane, passing through some gateposts where there is a signpost to Pendle.

2 In front of the house at Ing Ends, bear left. After a few paces, go right, through a metal kissing-gate. Follow this path, with the fence on your right, crossing a wooden stile. Go through the metal kissing-gate, then ahead.

3 Pass to the right of a corrugated barn, cross another stile and bear left, following the track uphill into a field. Go through a wooden gate by a metal farm gate, where there is a yellow waymark sign by the wall. Go uphill through the field, with the wall on your right, towards a group of farm buildings. Turn right behind the buildings, crossing a wooden stile. Go through the yard, over the cattle grid and take the path to your left uphill.

4 Go through a kissing-gate, and follow the steep path bearing right, up the side of Pendle Hill Ⓑ. At the top, turn left in front of a wall and stile to the Beacon, marked by a trig point on the summit.

5 Make your way downhill, keeping to the left of the ridge and the main path, following a faint path across the heather towards a stone cairn. Continue heading slightly downhill, to join a stony track cutting back left down the side of the hill. Bear right, through the kissing-gate, and at the end of the path, turn left onto the track and follow it to Barley Lane.

6 Turn right along the lane and, after a few paces, cross the stone step stile in the wall on your left. Cross the field, bearing half right to reach a house. Cross the wooden stile next to the house and turn left up a track. Walk past some houses on your left, go through a wooden gate and continue past Windy Harbour Farm to Higher Laithe Barn.

7 Turn right through the middle of a field. At the bottom, cross a wooden stile into a small, triangular field and follow a high wall on your right. Leave the field by a gate and turn to the right.

8 Cross a bridge, and turn right onto a track leading past Lower Black Moss Reservoir Ⓒ back to Barley, coming out opposite the post office. Turn left through the village and left again to return to the car park.

▼*In wet weather, the path from the summit of Pendle Hill becomes a stream. Waterproof boots are essential!*

▲*As you leave the village of Barley, where the walk starts, you can see Pendle Hill in the distance. From the top of the hill, there is a splendid view (left) back over the way you have come.*

raspberry. Pendle's core is composed of limestone and millstone grit, dating from the Carboniferous period. The first settlements here were during the Bronze Age and remains of their 3,000-year-old stone huts have been found.

SALT PIES

The name Pendle derives from the Celtic 'pen', meaning hill. Another intriguing name tells us more about the past. Salt Pie Farm, near Upper

Black Moss Reservoir, is named after the mounds of salt provided by Cheshire mines. The salt pies were delivered by packhorse to local farms, where the salt was used for preserving meat through the winter.

Windy Harbour Farm, on the site of a former deer enclosure, dates to the time when the area was appropriated as part of a royal deer forest.

'Brasts', or waterquakes, have, on occasion, burst Pendle's hillside open under the pressure of water.

the summit for the panoramic view it offers of coastline and hills, agricultural plains and the industrial landscape of the cotton towns.

The hill is bare of trees or bushes, but supports tough mountain grasses, clubmosses and cotton-grass, as well as the insect-catching butterwort. You may also find bilberry and cloudberry, a cousin of the

▶*From the summit of Pendle Hill, the Upper and Lower Black Moss Reservoirs are visible to the east.*

The Pendle Witches

The Pendle Witches and many of their supposed victims lived in the villages surrounding Pendle Hill. Foremost among the witches was Elizabeth Southernes, who was heartily feared as 'Old Mother Demdike'. Another ringleader was Anne Whittle, known as 'Old Chattox'. Their coven was made up

IT happened one time that a great number of Lancafhire Witches were reviling in a gentleman's houfe, in his abfence, and making merry with what they found, the dogs not daring to ftir, they having it feems, power to ftrike them

A crude illustration from a pamphlet of 1612, relating to the Pendle Witches. The witch is probably Old Mother Demdike.

of their disreputable families and neighbours. Despite the accounts of their misdeeds and trial, mystery still surrounds the true story.

King James I was ruthlessly determined to rid the country of witchcraft. Equally zealous was Lancashire magistrate, Roger Nowell of Read Hall. When Chattox, Demdike and some of their followers were arrested, they were put on trial in 1612, at Lancaster's grim castle. They were accused of causing the mysterious deaths of local people, ruining crops, souring ale and turning milk into butter. The two families hastened their own downfall by a series of accusations against each other.

It caused a sensation when Mistress Alice Nutter was arrested at the same time. She was a wealthy and refined woman, the widow of Richard Nutter of Roughlee Hall. She may only have been on her way to an illegal Catholic meeting, but to protect her friends, she died convicted of witchcraft. In all, 19 witches were tried, and 10 were found guilty. Old Mother Demdike, who was over 90, escaped the gallows only by dying in her cell.

▲*Where the route crosses Barley Lane on the way to Windy Harbour Farm, you cross a stone step stile into a field.*

contemplative silence for guidance.

Fox records in his diary that he climbed Pendle Hill 'with much ado', as it was so steep. On top of Pendle, he had a vision of a great number of people who were 'waiting to be gathered'. Modern-day Quakers often climb Pendle Hill in a spirit of pilgrimage.

East of Pendle Hill, the Black Moss reservoirs ● have been dug from beds of shale. They hold more than 100 million gallons (450 million litres), and provide water for the nearby town of Nelson. North West Water have planted forests around the reservoirs in the area, mainly of sitka, spruce and beech.

The worst of these created Brast Clough. These natural events were sometimes attributed to sorcery.

When the winter snows thaw, leaving the deep snow behind in the northern gullies, the shape of a witch is formed, complete with pointed hat and flowing robes — an eerie reminder of the superstitions surrounding this area.

SITE OF A VISION

In 1652, a little after the time of the notorious Pendle Witches (see box), Pendle was climbed by George Fox, founder of the Religious Society of Friends, or Quakers. The name 'Quakers' stems from an incident when George Fox, arrested for a breach of the peace while preaching, told the magistrate he should tremble at the name of the Lord.

▶*Lower Black Moss Reservoir, on the way back to Barley, is surrounded by fields providing rich pasture.*

George Fox was a Puritan who became disillusioned with organized religion and was dismayed by the less-than-Puritanical behaviour of some of his friends. He developed the idea of a religious service which involved waiting in

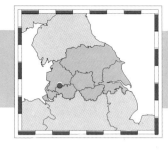

▲*Anglezarke Reservoir laps against a wooded shoreline that gives it a natural appearance. The red-throated diver (inset) is an interesting winter visitor to these waters. The whipping post (below right) is a reminder of school discipline in a different era.*

Exploring naturalized Victorian reservoirs on the edge of moorland

Known locally as the 'Little Lake District', the countryside around Anglezarke has been profoundly influenced by Liverpool's need for water. The series of 19th-century reservoirs here are among the most beautifully naturalized man-made features in the county.

During the winter months, they play host to a wide variety of waterfowl, including whooper swans, wigeon, tufted duck and the occasional diver and cormorant. Summer sees a multitude of songbirds nesting in the dense undergrowth that has been created by conservation-conscious rangers, while families of herons compete with hordes of anglers for fish.

The walk begins near the southern end of Anglezarke Reservoir, the second largest and perhaps the most interesting of them all, with many secluded corners that can only be reached by footpaths. A succession of wood anemones, bluebells, foxgloves and willowherbs line the banks, which are dotted at intervals with carrs (boggy copses) of alder and stunted oak trees.

WINTER DUCKS

Soon you come to an overflow channel known as the 'By-wash' Ⓐ. This leads from the higher Yarrow Reservoir, an open water that attracts plenty of ducks during the winter. After heavy rain, water tumbles noisily and with great force over a series of large steps. During the height of summer it may dry up almost completely.

From here, sandy lanes lead down to the edge of Rivington village. The primary school Ⓑ was previously the Free Grammar

---

FACT FILE

☀ Anglezarke, West Pennine Moors, 7 miles (11km) north-west of Bolton

▱ Pathfinder 700 (SD 61/71), grid reference SD 620160

miles 0 1 2 3 4 5 6 7 8 9 10 miles
kms 0 1 2 3 4 5 6 7 8 9 10 11 12 13 14 15 kms

◔ Allow 3½ hours

▬ Varied going across open moors and pastureland. One steep, grassy ascent

P Anglezarke Quarries, at start

🍴 Tea rooms at Rivington. Ice cream van often parked at start

I There is a Visitor Centre at Rivington, Tel. (01204) 691549

THE WALK

ANGLEZARKE – RIVINGTON – HIGH BULLOUGH RESERVOIR

The car park and picnic site at Anglezarke Quarries, where the walk begins, can be reached by following signposted by-roads from Adlington or Horwich.

1 Leave the car park by the access road and walk along a metalled lane, keeping the lake on your right-hand side. Turn right at a traffic island and continue until you reach a tiered overflow **A** on your left. Where the road bends sharply to the right, leave it to go through a gateway on your left. Walk along a bridleway that soon veers away to the right to join another stony bridleway that comes in from your left.

2 Bear right and follow this lane to its end. Climb a stone stile, and turn right along a metalled private road between two dry-stone walls. At the road junction, turn left to walk uphill, passing Rivington junior school **B**, and look out for a kissing-gate in the wall on the left, opposite

▼ *The track to Dean Wood is lined with rhododendrons, and is at its best in late spring when they are in bloom.*

School. Schoolchildren have come to school along these lanes for over four centuries, though the present building is just 270 years old. The whipping post visible in its court-yard dates from a bygone age.

The village green is flanked by ancient drinking troughs and crowned by a set of restored stocks. Beyond it, you turn onto a path and down a set of 39 steps to a wooded avenue. Most of the woods along the route are relatively young, having been established since the lakes were created in the middle of the 19th century. The notable exception is Dean Wood **C**, a jealously guarded remnant of ancient woodland in the depths of a plunging ravine.

The footpath affords an aerial view across the canopy of ash, oak and sycamore that hides the understorey of blackthorn, rowan and several other shrubs. The valley sides are so steep that the crowns of majestic ash trees are at eye level, only 30 feet (9m) away from you. Squirrels can be seen running through the tree tops and crows call from nests across the narrow gorge.

SECRET HAVEN

In the damp valley bottom, barely discernible through the hazel and bramble scrub, rare and luxuriant ferns, mosses, liverworts and fungi grow in almost total seclusion. Studied in detail only by the most

Rivington village green.

3 Go through the gate and follow a grass track across a field and down the 39 steps. Cross a stile and continue to another stile. Turn right through the gateway and follow a chestnut-lined lane to a stile into a field at the head of the track. Cross the stile and walk along the edge of the field, keeping the wire fence on your right. The nature reserve of Dean Wood **C** lies in the valley to your right. Cross a stile out of the field and walk along an enclosed footpath to a gateway at its end.

4 Turn left along a road. A steep descent leads to a bridge over Yarrow Reservoir. Cross it and turn right at the junction. Go through a gateway that leads onto a rough road, then cross a concrete bridge. Follow the path alongside a fast-flowing stream dotted with small waterfalls **D**. Recross the stream by means of a small concrete footbridge and turn right through a gate. Walk up the hill to the wartime memorial **E**.

5 Climb the steps over a

wall to your left. Follow the path uphill, leading straight across a field, to a wider farm track. Walk ahead through a gate and along the gravel path. Pass through a stile beyond a gate to join a tarmac road.

6 Turn right along the road. Walk downhill, curving left then bearing right as you skirt the perimeter wall of Manor House **F**. Opposite the house, go through a gateway on your left. Cross the field to a small gate into a wooded area. Keep to a narrow path down the steep slope through dense young woodland. When the path forks, bear right, following a 'Woodland Trail' signpost.

7 At the far end of the reservoir embankment, the path crosses a farm track and then continues going uphill. Follow the well-defined path round the headland and through a beechwood. On reaching a metalled road turn right. At a fork, bear left on a tarmac path through the disused quarry **G**. Take a left-hand fork uphill to return to the car park at the start.

▲ *The valley of the River Yarrow was the site of lead mining 300 years ago. On the moors above Limestone Clough is a memorial (below right) to a World War II bomber crew killed here.*

determined, permit-holding naturalists, the valley of Dean Wood does not give up its mysteries easily.

The route crosses the edge of Anglezarke Moor beneath Noon Hill, the site of a primordial burial ground. Today, hang gliders spiral earthwards from its summit when the weather is fine. The very name Anglezarke evokes a mysterious past for these bleak moorlands (it means 'Anuf's Heathen Temple') and, even now, primitive rituals are sometimes enacted on the moors.

You descend again, with Yarrow Reservoir sparkling below to your left, into the pleasant valley of Limestone Brook **D**, a swift-flowing moorland stream graced by several

small but attractive waterfalls. Dippers and grey wagtails dance from stone to stone chasing the many water-borne insects that mature in the stream.

LIMESTONE CLOUGH

Unlike Dean Wood, the valley, known as Limestone Clough, has been much marked by both sheep-farming and industry. The valley contains few mature trees, although stock-proof fencing has now been erected to counter the problem.

In the 17th century, lead was mined here. Several of the workings have been restored by conservation groups, and a waterwheel pit, pump shaft and many other relics can be

seen. Signposts and information boards will guide you around the small valley if you wish to leave the route to explore it.

A winding set of stone steps weaves up the hillside to a stone memorial **E**. It commemorates the crew of a Wellington bomber that crashed on the moorlands during World War II, killing all on board. The memorial is often decorated by floral wreaths and crosses.

The next section of footpath follows a straight track, thought to be

of Roman origin, leading to the Manor House **❻**, an imposing stone dwelling with decorative black and white barge boards. The age of this property is uncertain. A datestone confirms that extensions were added in 1604, but wattle and daub walls, recently uncovered within the stone structure, indicate that it has much earlier origins.

THE KNOLL

You now descend a steep, narrow path to the banks of the smallest and most secluded lake, High Bullough Reservoir. Shrouded by mature woodland, it resounds with bird calls at dusk and dawn, as woodpigeons coo from their perches and jays squabble raucously.

After skirting the northern edge of the reservoir, you climb a hill to a promontory known as the Knoll, which offers panoramic views of Anglezarke Reservoir. Flocks of Canada geese, gulls and herons can be watched going about their

business, unconcerned by your presence. Identification boards have been positioned at strategic points.

After emerging from a beech-wood, keep a look out on your left for the remnants of a cartwheel embedded in the trunk of a dying elm tree. Positioned over 100 years ago, reputedly to commemorate the opening of the quarry, the wheel has

▲*Now disused, Anglezarke Quarries were a handy local source of stone when the reservoirs were being built.*

rotted to the bare metal. This industrial monument has survived vandalism to this day, though the tree has recently succumbed to Dutch elm disease.

The quarry **❼**, long since abandoned to nature, was first worked to provide stone for the reservoir embankments, and was a major source of employment for the area. After the completion of the lakes, the stone was used to create millions of cobbles and kerbstones for the Manchester conurbation. The spoil heaps are now buried under masses of heather and bilberry, which provide a feast for local wildlife and serve to illustrate how well nature can repair man's scars. From here, a short walk leads you back to the car park at the start.

▼*Manor House, which has decorative woodwork on its gables, dates from 1604 but parts of it are even earlier.*

Making Lakes

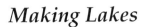

The 'Little Lake District' owes its existence to the continuous and accelerating growth of Liverpool in the late 19th century. In order to meet the needs of an ever expanding population, the city was forced to find and develop a substantial and reliable water supply.

The valleys of Anglezarke, on the moors to the north-east of the city, were quickly recognized as an ideal site for reservoirs to catch the water running down from the hills. Major engineering works began, and several rivers and streams were dammed.

Created nearly 150 years ago, the attractive Anglezarke Reservoir is the second largest body of water in the valley.

The first piped waters began to flow in the late 1850s. The project, one of the first of its kind to be undertaken, was hailed as a major success and became the model for similar water collection and storage systems all over the world.

The four 'lakes' (Anglezarke, Yarrow, High Bullough and Upper Rivington Reservoirs) filter through to the Lower Rivington Reservoir via sluices and channels, such as the By-wash overflow. On reaching the works in Horwich, at the southern end of the complex, they are treated and piped to Liverpool.

Many properties were submerged as the waters rose, perhaps the most notable being Lady Hall, a country mansion. The Black-a-Moor's Head in Rivington also disappeared, leaving the village without an inn to this day. The enterprising navvies did not go without a drink, however, as many unlicensed beer vendors and moonshine stills soon sprang up to meet the growing demand.

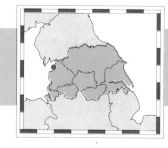

Wading birds and an old harbour at the mouth of the Lune

▲ *In the 18th century, the pretty Cotton Tree Cottage was the home of a Lancashire sea captain. The ringed plover (below) can often be seen on shingle shores and coastal mudflats.*

Sunderland Point lies at the end of a road that is buried under water at every high tide. Marshy inlets form part of the mouth of Lancashire's River Lune and, at low tide, the muddy channels are the rich feeding ground of numerous waders, which assemble in flocks to feed. The longer-legged waders include the oystercatcher, easily picked out by its black-and-white plumage and orange beak. Grey herons may be seen on the mudflats, standing still or flying with slow wing-beats and dangling legs.

BIRDWATCHERS' PARADISE

The car park at the start of the walk is an excellent spot from which to observe the bird life. At high tide, this area of shingly beach is often completely covered by the water, so be sure to time your walk correctly!

The cluster of cottages on this remote peninsula is a reminder of Lancashire's early trading days in the 17th century, when transatlantic ships sailed up the river Lune to Lancaster carrying sugar, tobacco, rum and ginger. The first wool of

the cotton plant was shipped here from America, as well as mahogany from the West Indies.

The Lune was not a good river for sea-going vessels, however, because of its numerous shoals and shallow water. A solution was to unload and load ships at Sunderland Point, at the mouth of the river. Cotton wool was stored in warehouses, which have since been converted into cottages. The sailors, anchored offshore, nicknamed the harbour Cape Famine, as there was not even a pub here to provide amusement.

Some of the profits from the

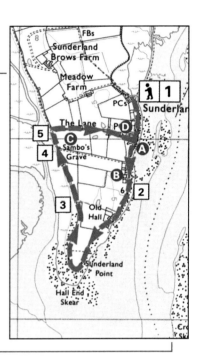

THE WALK

SUNDERLAND – SUNDERLAND POINT

The walk begins on the shingle car park at the end of the road that leads from Overton to Sunderland.

1 Follow the stony lane from the car park past the houses and cottages that lie along the water's edge. Continue walking along the edge of the harbour, past the old 'cotton tree' **A**

growing from the base of Cotton Tree Barn. Walk by the single gatepost, and then past some more houses to come to Sunderland Hall **B**.

2 From Sunderland Hall, continue on the shore around the Point.

3 Walk along a shingle path that runs between the estuarial marshes on the left and fields on the right.

4 Just before a bench,

follow a signpost marked 'Sambo' over a stone stile into a field. Sambo's Grave **C** is marked by a plaque 50 feet (15m) inside the field.

5 Continue along the shore for about 100 yards (90m). Turn right through a wooden gate onto a bridleway called The Lane to return to the village, passing Upsteps Cottage **D**. Turn left along the harbour's edge to return to the car park.

▲ *The tides control the movement not only of pleasure boats but also of cars and pedestrians at Sunderland Point.*

extensive trading with Africa, America and the West Indies went into many fine Georgian buildings in Lancaster. The estuary was gradually silting up, however, and, towards the end of the 18th century, Sunderland Point was superseded by Glasson Dock on the opposite bank. In the early 1800s, Sunderland was popular as a bathing place, but with the coming of the railway it was overtaken by Morecambe.

COTTON TREE COTTAGE

Along the edge of the old harbour stands Cotton Tree Cottage, which was once the home of a Lancaster sea captain. Next to it is Cotton Tree Barn, a substantial stone building that has been converted into a house. From the base of the wall grows a gnarled old 'cotton tree' **A**, which is actually a black poplar, whose seeds resemble cotton.

Just beyond it is Sunderland Hall **B**, an elegant, colonial-style house with verandahs, which dates from

1683. It was the family home of Robert Lawson, a Quaker merchant, who first had the idea of using Sunderland Point as an extension to the port of Lancaster.

There is a lane along the harbour's edge, but beyond Sunderland Hall the walk continues on the shingle and sand of the foreshore around the headland. Along the shoreline, yellow broom and pink wild thyme flourish, and black-headed gulls fly overhead. Around the Point, a rough track runs alongside the salt marshes, another good bird-spotting area. Ahead, Heysham's nuclear power plant is a reminder of the 20th century. Beyond, there are views of the hills of the Lake District across Morecambe Bay.

A little distance along the sandy track that runs between the estuarial marshes and fields, a wooden signpost marked 'Sambo' points to a field, where you find Sambo's Grave **C**, marked by a plaque. Sambo was a black slave, who accompanied his master, a sea captain, to England. Soon after they arrived at Sunderland Point in 1735, Sambo died, probably from a fever

that he had contracted earlier.

As Sambo was a heathen, he could not be buried in consecrated ground, but was interred in the corner of a field, far from the sunny climes of his homeland. In 1796, a master of Lancaster Grammar School held a collection to raise money for a plaque to mark the grave. He also composed a poem, and three verses were put on the plaque, the last of which reads:

But still he sleeps —
till the awakening sounds
Of the archangel's trump
new life impart
Then the Great Judge
his approbation founds
Not on man's colour,
but his worth of heart.

A little further on is a gate and bridleway leading back to the village. It emerges at the end of Second Terrace. Sambo died in the loft of Upsteps Cottage **D**, the stone cottage with steps outside.

▼ *Upsteps Cottage, where the black slave Sambo died, is not much visited.*

MOORS AND MILLS

◀ *The ruined chimney of the scrubbing mill and its surrounding quarries now lie silent. Today, the gritstone is used only in dry-stone walls, which are often covered with lichens (inset).*

A moorland walk in a former textile area above Helmshore

This is a scenic walk through millstone grit country, above the mill towns of Lancashire. In between the millstone grit are beds of softer shale, which erode more easily; this creates the spectacular landscape seen today.

The first part of the route goes uphill past sturdy, stone farms and rough pasture. Farming has always been important here, although the land has never been very fertile. Oats, beans and peas were grown in the valleys, and small farmers kept pigs and poultry, but most of the area was devoted to cattle and sheep. Bigger landowners also bred horses. Today, hardy Dalesbred sheep graze the rough pastures.

Most families needed to find work to supplement the meagre income

they derived from agriculture. Only larger landowners were able to make a profit from their land; most other, smaller farmers had to be content with growing enough just to

FACT FILE

⚹ Helmshore, 7 miles (11.2km) south-east of Blackburn, on the B6235

▱ Pathfinder 689 (SD 62/72), grid reference SD 777214

miles 0 1 2 3 4 5 6 7 8 9 10 miles
kms 0 1 2 3 4 5 6 7 8 9 10 11 12 13 14 15 kms

◖ 3 hours

▬ Stony tracks and narrow moorland paths, which can be boggy or muddy. Some long, fairly steep ascents and descents. Strong walking boots or shoes recommended

P Car park at the start

T Local BR train service to Accrington

🏰 Helmshore Textile Museum, Tel. (01706) 226459 for details. The museum has a café and toilets

🍴

WC

I For tourist information, Tel. (01706) 226590

live on. Extra work was provided on a small scale by quarrying. In the 19th century it became a major industry; thousands of tons of stone dug out at Musbury Heights Ⓐ made setts, kerbs and flagstones for Lancashire's streets.

The walk passes through the spoil heaps of the old quarry. The chimney remains are part of the scrubbing mill, where flagstones were dragged round and round to smooth their surface. The finished stone was brought down the hillside in tubs supported by a steel rope, on a long, straight incline.

The immediate area flourished until the turn of the 20th century, when it fell victim to the growing demand for drinking water from the mill towns below. Three reservoirs Ⓑ were created here, and the hillside was depopulated to ensure the purity of the run-off water.

MOORLAND BIRDS

Beyond the quarry is moorland, where you may spot skylarks and curlews. There are colourful lichens on the grey gritstone walls, and various types of mosses in the banks. The acid, peaty soil of the moor supports tussocks of tough grasses, mosses and rushes. All along the way are the crumbled ruins of farmhouses abandoned when the Ogden Reservoir was built.

The path runs along a bank next to a deep gully, part of the boundary of the old Musbury Deer Park Ⓒ. The park was enclosed in 1304 on the orders of Henry de Lacy, then Lord of the Manor. The area was reserved for hunting until Tudor times, when tenants were encouraged to lease and farm the lands.

In the 16th century, people earned extra money by spinning, bleaching and weaving wool in their homes, and selling the cloth. The trade involved almost every family on the moorlands of Lancashire. Later,

MUSBURY TOR

The walk starts from the car park of Helmshore Textile Museums.

1 Turn right and follow the road for about ¼ mile (400m). At the end of a row of cottages, Park Lane View, turn very sharp left up a track signposted to Musbury Heights. Go along the track for a short distance behind the cottages, then bear right up a grassy lane towards a gate. Cross the stile and continue uphill along a grassy track, which swings round to the right to pass a ruined farmhouse. At another wooden farm gate, cross the stile next to it and turn right along a track. Keep left of a farm, and continue along a narrow track with a wall on its left. At the end of the wall, continue in the same direction (pointed by a waymark arrow) and join a broad track.

2 Where the track bends right towards a farm, take another track ahead to a metal gate. Go through and bear right to follow the track uphill. Go through a metal gate, and continue along a track through Musbury Heights Quarry **A** for about 50 yards (45m). The reservoirs **B** are below you.

3 Turn left to follow the waymarked Rossendale Way through the spoilheaps of the quarry.

4 Leave the quarry by a stone stile set into the dry- stone wall and go ahead, along the moorland path. Soon, the path runs next to a gully, which was the boundary of the Musbury Deer Park **C**. After about 1 mile (1.6km), at the head of the valley, the path veers left and crosses three streams to reach the far side of the valley.

5 Continue slightly uphill along the narrow valley path until it eventually widens. Cross a wooden step stile next to a waymarked metal gate. Cross the next field, and go through another waymarked gate in the stone wall. Continue through a gate, down the hill towards a farm.

6 At the next gate, before the farm, leave the Rossendale Way and bear left alongside a wall on your right, with Musbury Tor **D** on your left. Continue over a stone step stile and head downhill. Cross a ladder stile over the wall ahead.

7 Turn sharp right and walk downhill, with the wall on your right. Cross another stile and turn left along a track. Go through the white metal gate ahead, and follow a faint track across the field. Go through the narrow gap in the wall. Head downhill across the field, towards the mill chimney, to a walled track at the bottom. Turn right and follow the track to the road (B6235). Turn left back to the textile museums **E**.

mills were built in the valleys, and people moved off the high moors in search of work.

The last stage of the walk leads over the shoulder of the prominent round hill of Musbury Tor **D**, and returns along a walled green lane, an old packhorse route. Two mills have been converted into textile museums **E**. Higher Mill was built in 1789 for 'fulling', a process where wool is beaten to interlock its fibres.

In the 18th century, cotton began to arrive from America. Whitaker's Mill was built next to Higher Mill to spin cotton after Arkwright's water frame made large-scale power spinning a possibility. The working museum contains early examples of textile machinery, including Hargreaves's Spinning Jenny.

BLACKSTONE EDGE

The wild moorland on the edge of industrial Manchester

Within view of the industrial satellites of Manchester, the jagged ridge of Blackstone Edge marks the summit of an ancient route into West Yorkshire. To the south is the M62 motorway but here you can enjoy peace and solitude. For much of the year the cries of moorland birds can be heard and there are some fine views over Littleborough and Rochdale.

DAUNTING CROSSING

This wild moorland walk traces the history of road transport over the Pennines. The route over Blackstone Edge was used in the past by trains of pack-horses and later by wagons and carriages. Daniel Defoe, who wrote *Robinson Crusoe*, followed the route on a wild winter's day early in the 18th century and found it a daunting crossing.

The walk starts from the historic White House pub **Ⓐ**, once a coaching inn, where teams of horses were changed and passengers rested. The

▲ *The grassy moorland path leading across Blackstone Edge, a famous trans-Pennine pass. These high, moorland passes are the perfect habitat for the Alpine lady's mantle (right).*

FACT FILE

✳ Blackstone Edge, on the crest of the Pennines, lies between the M62 and the A58

🗺 Outdoor Leisure Map 21, South Pennines, grid reference SD 968178

miles 0 1 2 3 4 5 6 7 8 9 10 miles
kms 0 1 2 3 4 5 6 7 8 9 10 11 12 13 14 15 kms

◗ Allow 2 hours

▬ A walk on moorland tracks and a series of old roads (muddy in places) with a 650-foot (200-metre) ascent

🍴 The White House and the Moorcock Inn 1 mile (1.6 km) towards Littleborough. There is
WC a café at the visitor centre at Hollingworth Lake Country Park

A58 follows the line of a turnpike toll road built in the 1790s. Some of the tall stones that marked the line of the road through winter snows are still in position. Below the A58, forming part of the walk, runs an earlier coach road **Ⓑ**. Today it is a grassy terrace on the hillside. It was built in the late 1760s and replaced by a newer road on the line of the A58. Beside the old road are many small, overgrown quarries, which provided material for road making. The largest, the Blue Delf **Ⓒ**, has been flooded to form an attractive pond. The Stormer Hill Toll-house **Ⓓ**, where the old road rejoins the A58, was once a turnpike toll-house.

The track that comes down to the cottages at Lydgate **Ⓔ** was formerly the main pack-horse road over Blackstone Edge. It has been deeply

THE WALK

BLACKSTONE EDGE

Begin at the car park by the White House pub **A**.

1 From the car park follow the bridlepath sign down the grassy track that runs just below the A58. This track used to be part of the old coach road **B**. It runs past several disused quarries, including the flooded Blue Delf **C**.

2 Cross the A58 at Stormer Hill Toll-house **D** and follow the minor road to Lydgate.

3 At Lydgate **E** turn left just after bridge and follow the track that runs in front of the row of cottages. Follow the path beyond the cottages, keeping the stone wall to your right.

4 Just before you reach the A58 the path crosses a metalled track. Immediately beyond, turn right to follow the line of the Roman road **F** that makes directly for the crest of Blackstone Edge.

5 At the Aiggin Stone **G** turn left onto a narrow footpath. This broadens out along an old section of pack-horse road **H**, which curves gently downhill until it reaches the drain from Blackstone Edge Reservoir.

6 Cross the drain by a concrete footbridge and turn right along the broad footpath on the far side. Follow this around the hillside until you are back at the White House.

◄Blue Delf pond is a flooded quarry. The stone was used to build the pack-horse road (below). The groove was either for turf to help horses grip or as a channel for ropes to winch carts up.

hollowed in places by centuries of traffic. The road that climbs towards the summit of the pass is very different though. As the slope steepens there are smooth, round cobbles among the peat and turf. Higher up, the full extent of this fine, paved roadway **F** becomes evident.

Of all the old roads around Blackstone Edge, this one has aroused the most controversy. On the map, it is marked as a Roman road and many textbooks refer to it as the best preserved section of Roman road in Britain. There are, though, serious doubts about its age. Halfway up the slope there is a passing place where a medieval pack-horse track passes under the causeway. This suggests the road is relatively recent — possibly a turnpike from the 1760s, which was abandoned due to its steep gradient.

FACTORY CHIMNEYS

At the summit of the pass the causeway and pack-horse road meet at the Aiggin Stone **G**, an upright block with a worn, crudely incised cross. This is a good place to pause for breath and admire the view of the distant factory chimneys of industrial Lancashire and the long line of gritstone outcrops that marks Blackstone Edge proper, which lie a short distance above them.

The Aiggin Stone was one of many wayside route markers on the medieval pack-horse track. The section of the walk down from the Aiggin Stone to the reservoir drain follows a well-preserved section of this pack-horse road **H**.

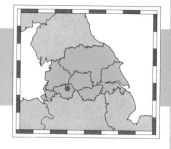

The large number of paths and tracks that criss-cross the hills and valleys are evidence of the area's past importance. This walk sets out along some of these routes, past Wolstenholme Fold **B**, a collection of cottages and farms typical of the West Pennines. This was once home to a community of farmer-weavers, who supplied part-finished cloth to

◀ *In the valley of Naden Brook, a disused chimney of an old textile mill is a reminder of the industry that once thrived here. An alert fox (below) may well be seen at some point on the walk.*

FACT FILE

✳ Cheesden, 5 miles (8km) north-west of Rochdale on the A680

🗺 Pathfinder 701 (SD 81/91), grid reference SD 829160

miles 0 1 2 3 4 5 6 7 8 9 10 miles
kms 0 1 2 3 4 5 6 7 8 9 10 11 12 13 14 15 kms

◔ Allow 4 hours

▬ Gentle climbs and one short, steep scramble. Woods, pastures and moorland tracks. Some marshy sections and several sets of rough stepping-stones

P Opposite and next to Owd Betts pub

T Infrequent bus service between Rochdale and Rawtenstall, Tel. (0161) 228 7811

🍴 Owd Betts pub, and New Inn at Cheesden

Remains of a small-scale industry in spectacular wooded gorges

The West Pennine Moors loom like a huge wall across the top of the great basin containing Manchester and its satellite towns. Owd Betts pub **A**, where the walk begins, is situated on the edge of the moorland. On a clear day, there are views south and east to the Cheshire Plain and Derbyshire Peaks and you can see the white dish of Jodrell Bank's radio telescope and the mountains of North Wales.

WATER POWER

In the foreground, Ashworth Moor Reservoir, one of many created in this area to serve the nearby towns, is visible at the foot of Knowl Hill. Over the past two centuries, the valleys and the water have been exploited to drive mills for the production of cloth and paper.

THE WALK

CHEESDEN – NADEN BROOK – CHEESDEN BROOK

The walk commences at Owd Betts pub Ⓐ, Cheesden, 5 miles (8km) north-west of Rochdale on the A680.

1 With the pub on your left, walk along the road towards Rochdale. After 300 yards (270m), angle right along a rough track that runs past a ruined barn. Cross a minor road and continue to a bungalow. Follow the rough drive to a public footpath sign pointing directly at you. Take the track behind it and wind round the crest of the small hill. Go through a white-painted, metal field gate and walk down the green lane, continuing beyond this to the cottages at Top o' th' Hill Farm. Past these, bear left with the lane then right at a junction. Continue to Marcroft Gate Farm.

2 Pass the farmhouse to your right, go through a gate and cross the yard, passing a white cottage. Turn left, go through a gate and keep the fence on your left for 50 paces. Bear right by a tree and follow a wall to the far side of the field. Turn left and keep the fence on your right. Climb a stile and bear right around a wire-meshed enclosure. Follow the stream to your right. Pass through an old gate, keep left of some beech trees and cross a field to come to a stone gatepost.

3 Turn left through a field and cross a double stile. Head for a cottage then go through a gap, to keep left of the garden wall. Cross a yard between a house and a barn, then go left along a drive, bearing sharp left and crossing a wooden-railed bridge over a stream. Follow the surfaced lane to Wolstenholme Fold Ⓑ. Keep right of Schofield Farm and follow the winding path down between steep banks to reach the remains of Coal Bank Mill.

4 Cross a footbridge and turn left. As the track bends right, take the second path from the right, gradually ascending the valley of Naden Brook Ⓒ. At the metalled School Lane, turn left then right after 50 yards (45m) at a

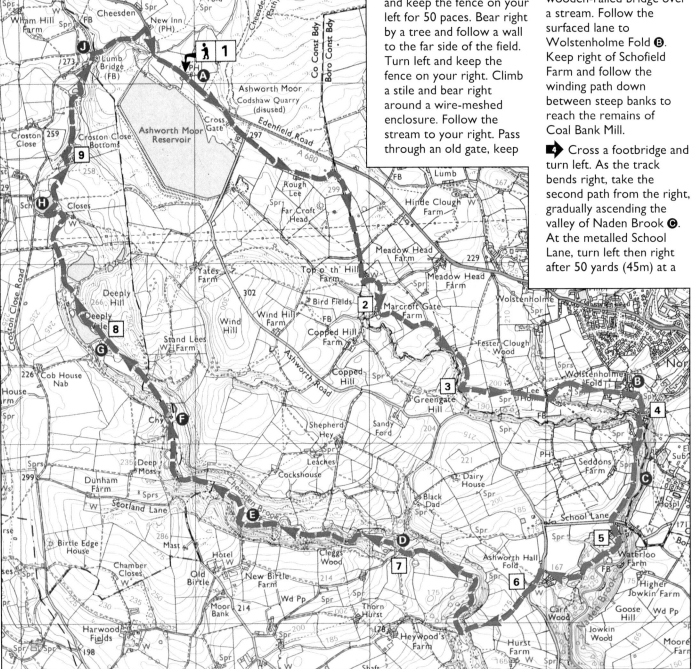

footpath sign. Follow the track to the left of a cottage, into woodland.

5 Go through a gate, past an old barn on your right. After about 150 yards (140m), bear right at a fork. The path soon narrows. Fork right again and climb a small stile beyond some holly bushes. At a minor road, turn left along it to walk through Ashworth Hall Fold.

6 Where the road bears sharp left, follow the signed rough drive on your right to its end. Cross a stile and continue. Cross another stile and enter the woods. At the foot of the slope, turn right on a cross path and follow it over a brook

via stepping stones. At a clearing, take the narrow path alongside a barbed-wire fence on your left. Bear right as the path becomes wider and walk up to, then along, the ridge above the valley. Go through a gap stile at the end and turn right to walk down a rough drive.

7 Just before a gate into the grounds of Nab's Wife **D**, take the steep, narrow bridleway on the right towards the river. Bear left along a path just above the water. Keep on the left side of the river and walk upstream for ½ mile (800m) to the large bowl surrounding Birtle Dean Mill **E**. Continue following the riverside path to a stile

over a fence, then cross the marshy field to the chimney at Lower Wheel **F**. Cross a bridge and turn left, walking between the brook and the chimney. Follow a distinct path leading beyond the ponds, then up the hillside on your right. When you reach a wide track, turn left to come to Deeply Vale **G**.

8 Follow the rough road along the right of a large pond, and up to the crest to the left of the next pond. Walk towards a squat pylon ahead, passing through a gap stile then following the stream towards a cottage at the far side of the field. Climb the stile and turn left along the drive. Just before a

cattle grid, turn back right along the top of the dam **H**. Cross the bridge and turn left. Cross a stile 50 yards (45m) beyond a stunted tree and continue up the valley.

9 Once above a waterfall, cross the old dam wall to the left-hand side of the valley and continue up through mill remains and some marshy areas to reach the facade of Cheesden Lumb Lower Mill **J**. Immediately behind this, cross a concrete footbridge, go through a kissing gate and continue up the valley. Go through a gate and turn right along the main road (A680), passing the New Inn to return to Owd Betts pub.

◀Throughout the walk, long-neglected industrial buildings are rapidly being overtaken by nature. This old mill stands at School Lane near Naden Brook. The chimney at Lower Wheel (right) was part of a bleaching works by Cheesden Brook (below right).

the small mills in the narrow valleys here. The remains of two of the mills can still be found in the valley of Naden Brook **C**. Part of the facade of Ashworth Mill stands in a gloomy, wooded hollow below a weir.

18TH-CENTURY MILL

In the neighbouring valley of Cheesden Brook are more remains. Kershaw Bridge Mill, founded in 1780, was the first mill recorded in the valley. It produced fustian, a hard-wearing mix of cotton and linen. It closed towards the end of

the 19th century, but the overseer's house, Nab's Wife **D**, still stands and is now a private house. Its name is a corruption of 'Nab's Wharfe'.

Birtle Dean Mill **E** stood further upstream in a great natural amphitheatre. Built in 1824, this substantial mill, the valley's largest, took in new cotton and produced dyed, finished cloth. Terraces of houses were built for its workers. It lasted less than 80 years; today, only a few stones and slabs remain. On hot summer days these are occupied by lizards and slow-worms, basking in the heat. In the 1960s, the site was used for outdoor pop concerts.

Beyond Birtle Dean, the valley loses its thick cover of trees and the valley widens out. The walk winds past shale terraces that mark the site of one of several mines in the valley. These were developed to produce coal for the steam engines that augmented or replaced the earliest of the mills' water wheels.

OLD MILLPONDS

Further on you pass a chimney-stack at Lower Wheel **F**, where there was once a bleaching works. The wide valley floor here is home to a large number of rabbits, easy prey for the foxes and buzzards that you may see here, along with white hares in winter.

The ruins of Deeply Vale **G**, a calico printing works which later produced paper, are more substantial than most: moss-covered, cobbled roads wind in and out of the woodland; walls covered by ivy

and ferns stand against the ravages of nature and vandals; and old, rust-stained wheel pits host large trees. The dam holds back a large millpond, now fringed by reeds and a favourite haunt of herons, coots and brightly coloured dragonflies.

For about the next mile (1.6km), the only reminders of the half dozen or so mills that once thrived here are a couple of dark, brooding ponds,

▼This waterfall on Cheesden Brook tumbles through the remains of a dam wall. Further up the valley you come to the facade (above) of Cheesden Lumb Lower Mill, once a wool mill.

Farmers and Weavers

The high moors around the Cheesden Valley have never been well suited to agriculture. Farmers have traditionally found life hard here, and in the 18th and 19th centuries many were forced to become part-time textile workers to supplement their meagre incomes.

Employed as outworkers or selling direct at local markets, they produced home-spun cloth. Wool and cotton were worked on small hand looms, washed in the moorland

A view of the weaving shed in a 19th-century Manchester cotton mill. The textile industry was once a major source of employment.

pools and streams, and pegged out on tenterhooks to dry, cure and bleach in the sun and wind.

This cottage industry was industrialized with the introduction of new machines towards the end of the 18th century. The West Pennines made an ideal site. The high rainfall on the tops plunged to the lowlands through narrow, steep valleys that were ideal locations for modest-sized mills. The weaver-farmers provided the manpower, and the plentiful sheep the raw materials. Later, Lancashire-produced flax, and imported or waste cotton, were also used.

On an essentially human scale, these early mills specialized in part-processing cloth at various stages of manufacture. Some were spinning mills and some bleaching works, while others specialized in printing or dyeing. All were a far cry from the mills of the later Victorian era, where all the processes were carried out on a single, vast site.

an occasional piece of masonry or cobbled path and the breached dams of several more millponds. Looking west from the dam at Longlands **H**, there is a fine view of Peel Tower above Ramsbottom and of the distant Winter Hill above Bolton. The building in the foreground was Buckhurst School, provided by the mill owners.

STORM DAMAGE

Across the top of the narrow valley stretches the impressive facade of Cheesden Lumb Lower Mill **J**. This old wool mill was badly damaged by a storm in 1990, but work funded by English Heritage has since led to its partial restoration.

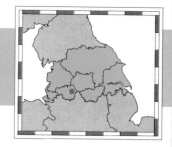

◄*At the Wool Road Transhipment Shed, where the walk starts, goods were once unloaded from narrowboats and saddled to packhorses. The merlin (below left) hunts on the moors.*

FACT FILE

✳ Uppermill, 4 miles (6.4km) east of Oldham on the A670

▱ Pathfinders 713 (SD 80/90) and 714 (SE 00/10), grid reference SD 995066

🕐 Allow 4 to 5 hours

🌉 Some steep ascents and descents on roads, moorland paths and tracks. Riverside and towpaths can be boggy

Ⓟ Wool Road Car Park at the start

Ⓣ Buses to Brownhills Visitor Centre from Manchester, Oldham, Ashton-under-Lyne and Huddersfield, Tel. (0161) 228 7811

🍴 Church Inn and Cross Keys, Saddleworth; Horse and Jockey Inn, Castle Shaw; several pubs in the villages. Cafés in Diggle, Delph and Dobcross

Ⓘ Brownhills Visitor Centre, open Tues-Sun, Tel. (01457) 872598

native-born Yorkshiremen, eligible to play for the county's cricket team. Throughout this walk, there are reminders of the industrial heritage that created these communities on the moorland edge.

The walk starts by the Wool Road Transhipment Shed Ⓐ. Bales of wool, worsted, cotton and other

▼*Behind the Brownhills Visitor Centre a railway viaduct straddles the canal.*

Exploring gritstone villages on the edge of Saddleworth Moor

S addleworth, on the upper reaches of the River Tame in the north-east corner of Greater Manchester, is a typical gritstone village. Until 1974, this was part of the West Riding of Yorkshire, and men born in the area are still considered

THE WALK

WOOL ROAD – CASTLE SHAW – DELPH

The walk begins at the car park by the Wool Road Transhipment Shed **A**.

1 Walk south along the towpath, with the canal **B** on your right, to the Visitor Centre **C**. Retrace your steps, then cross the A670 to a turning circle. Take the rough lane to the right of the garden gate to house No. 20. At a hairpin bend, continue ahead along a grassy path to a railway line. Cross the line with care. Follow the waymarked path, through the gates, up the hillside to a narrow road.

2 Go straight on with cottages on your left. At a bend, go straight ahead along a driveway towards Ryefields. Take a signposted footpath right, through the fence and down to a lower road. Turn left, and continue for about ¾ mile (1.2km), going through a gap stile and crossing a beck. At a fork just beyond a pond on your left, bear right to a road and turn right to the church **D**.

3 Go back down the

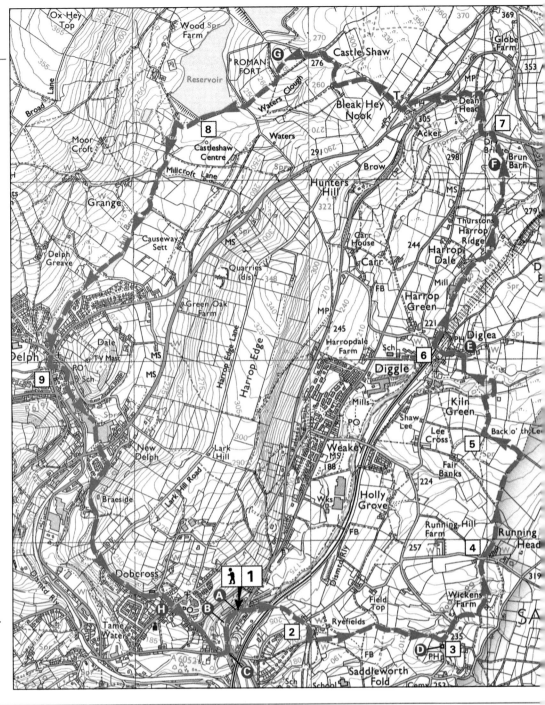

▼ *These village stocks, supported by stone posts in St Chad's churchyard, Saddleworth, are over 300 years old.*

goods from Manchester were once unloaded from narrowboats here, and transferred to strings of packhorses, which took them over the Pennines. The packhorse traffic lasted just 12 years, from the opening of the Huddersfield Narrow Canal **B** in 1799 to the completion of the Standedge Tunnel, which took the boats through the moors, in 1811.

VICTORIAN CHURCH

You cross the canal near the Brownhills Visitor Centre **C**, which provides information about the region's natural history, and climb gradually towards Saddleworth's parish church, St Chad's **D**, on the hillside high above the village. It marks the site of the original hamlet, built when the valley below was still well wooded. The current gritstone building is a Victorian replacement for the Norman church founded here in 1200.

In the churchyard, a gravestone bears an inscription recording the brutal 19th-century murder of a pub landlord and his son. The killer was never caught, but the funeral drew an audience of around 10,000, swelled by the intense interest generated by the regional press; upwards of 30,000 people are said to have visited the scene of the killings within days of the event.

road and continue round a sharp, left-hand bend. Take the second drive on the right by a broken footpath sign. Walk up behind a white cottage to the concreted part of the drive to your right. This leads to a narrow, walled footpath. Go through two stiles at the top and walk up the sunken track. About 50 yards (45m) before a ruined farm, there is a stile on your right and a waymark arrow on your left. Turn left to pass below the ruins and cross the bridge and continue over a boggy field to a ladder stile, slightly to your right, onto a narrow road.

4 Turn right, then almost immediately left along a narrow, signposted footpath. Maintain your direction, ignoring a path off to your left, over a stile and along field edges until a walled greenway crosses. Turn left along it and head for some isolated cottages.

5 Go through a white gate beyond the cottages, turn sharp right and follow a wall on your right. Pass through a gap and walk half-left to the bottom of the field to a stile near a telegraph pole. Turn sharp right around the edge of a rough enclosure, and go through a wooden gate at the bottom. Turn left, cross the stream and pass through the bridleway gate at the far side of the paddock. Bear slightly right to a yellow metal gate, remaining with the path beyond this to Diglea **E**. Turn left down a road and follow it over a railway bridge.

6 Turn right along Harrop Court Road. At a 'No through road' sign, bear right to the entrance to Harrop Court Farm. Go straight ahead up a short grassy track to the left of a barn, and through a gap stile by a gate on your left. Walk to the footbridge beneath the trees, cross and look ahead to a narrow, fenced-off valley. Pass through the fence via a wire-mesh gate, and bear half right. Follow the path up past a thorny tree, through the broken wall and then uphill alongside it to Brun Barn **F**. Just beyond is a homemade footpath sign. Climb the stile and walk beside the fence to the drive. Follow this to the road.

7 Turn left along the road. After about 100 yards (90m), just before a left-hand bend, turn right down a rough road. Where the A62 crosses, continue opposite along the green lane. Turn left at the end. Go down the surfaced road for 100 yards (90m), then turn right along the road between the houses, just before the post-box. Follow this road until you pass Castleshaw House on your right. Just round the corner is a gate on your left to the old Roman Fort **G**. Leave through a gap in the fence at the southern corner, just beyond an information plaque about an auxiliary infantryman. Follow an old wall towards the farm below. Go through the field gate left of the garden and turn right along the lower roadway, following this onto the dam.

8 Where the road bears right halfway across the dam, go down the steps on the left and through a stile. Cross the long wooden footbridge down to your right. Turn left and walk to another footbridge. Recross the brook and follow it downstream on the left bank. Cross a minor road and continue.

At a large millpond on your left, continue straight ahead past a bridleway sign down the valley, with new houses on your left. Bear left and pass another pond on your right. Follow the path behind the new houses to emerge by the White Lion Inn in Delph. Turn right. At a crossroads, go straight ahead along the main street to a river bridge.

9 Cross the bridge. Turn left on the riverside path. At a red factory gate, cross a footbridge and follow the river downstream to a mill yard. Bear right through this, with the river still on your right. Go through an arch beneath an old stone warehouse ahead and straight across the road. Follow Gate Head Road, opposite, all the way to the centre of Dobcross **H**, in front of The Swan Inn. Go straight on, with the pub on your left, and follow Sugar Lane out of the village. When the road bends left, bear right down Nicker Brow to some railings. Follow the steep footpath beyond these to a main road. Turn left to the junction beside Brownhills Visitor Centre, and retrace your steps along the towpath to the start.

Further on is the hamlet of Diglea **E**, a glorious survival of weavers' cottages and yeomen's houses, which once had several mills. Just to the north lies Standedge Canal Tunnel, which is now disused. At over 3 miles (5km), it is the longest (as well as the highest) in Britain.

Following Harrop Brook, the walk becomes gradually steeper. At Brun Barn **F**, there are extensive views down the Tame Valley. Ahead

◀ *Yeomen's houses and weavers' cottages can still be seen in Diglea. Just beyond Castle Shaw are earthworks (right) that once formed part of a Roman encampment.*

and to your right is a spoil tip topped by a large circular brick structure. This marks the course of the railway tunnel; the bricks are the top of a ventilation shaft.

Behind the Horse and Jockey Inn, the walk reaches its highest point, at around 1,000 feet (300m), before descending gradually to the site of Castleshaw Roman Fort **G**. This lonely, windswept outpost of the Roman Empire was commissioned

▼ *Castleshaw Reservoir attracts a variety of wildfowl. The gritstone buildings of Dobcross (right), and its steep main street, have featured in a well-known TV bread advertisement.*

by Agricola about AD79 and abandoned in AD120. Little remains, but information boards detail the history of the site.

The route crosses a reservoir dam and then passes two millponds. These waters are very popular with a variety of waterbirds, as well dragonflies in summer.

To the south of the village of Delph, set in a deep valley, is Shore Mill, a scribbling mill where raw wool was combed to make it easier to work. You climb along Harrop Edge to reach Dobcross **H**, the oldest village in the area. Its maze of back lanes and passages was used in the Hollywood film *Yanks* and, more recently, in a well-known TV bread advertisement. If any place typifies a Pennine gritstone village in all its glory, this is it.

Rushbearing

Each August Bank Holiday weekend, the Saddleworth area comes to a virtual standstill as the locals celebrate the Longwood Thrump Rushcart Festival.

This revival of a medieval fair harks back to the days when most churches and chapels had floors made of compressed earth or clay. As a celebration of the annual cycle of the renewal of the seasons, local people gathered rushes to strew over the floor of the church. This had the dual purpose of giving thanks and refreshing the atmosphere of the church; furthermore, it provided warm, dry flooring! Before they were spread, the rushes were paraded to every corner of the parish to ensure the spirit of renewal was shared by all.

The ceremonies were usually held either at the time of the first hay cutting or on the church's Patronage Day, the day dedicated to the saint after whom the church is named. Such rushbearing festivals were once commonplace, but most died out during Victorian times as churches were rebuilt and new floors laid. There was also a prevailing spirit of intolerance at that time of any practices that smacked of the pagan.

Today, the revived Longwood Thrump is a vast celebration centred on a beautifully rush-bedecked and decorated haywain, which is paraded through all the villages in Saddleworth by teams of locals before a service at St Chad's. It is claimed that the saying 'going on the wagon' (steering clear of alcohol) originates here — the balance and skill that are needed to climb onto and stay on the rushcart proscribes any consumption of beer, cider or spirits!

The Longwood Thrump Rushcart Festival, a revival of a medieval fair, is an annual event in the Saddleworth district.

A country ramble around the empire of a Georgian industrialist

▲*Marple Locks, a flight of 16 narrow locks, run between the attractive gardens of canalside houses. The ruffe (inset) is a small fish found in canals and slow-flowing rivers.*

Set squarely within Greater Manchester, with its beginning and end in suburbia, this is a surprisingly rural walk. It winds along the wooded banks of a canal before climbing to the bleak escarpment of Cobden Edge, where there is a fine

▼*The gently curved path that crosses bridge No. 19 allowed narrowboat horses to be led to the opposite towpath.*

FACT FILE

✳ Marple, 4 miles (6.4km) east of Stockport, on the A626

▭ Pathfinders 724 (SJ 89/99) and 741 (SJ 88/98), grid reference SJ 963892

miles 0 1 2 3 4 5 6 7 8 9 10 miles
kms 0 1 2 3 4 5 6 7 8 9 10 11 12 13 14 15 kms

◔ Allow 4 hours

▬ Towpath, moorland paths, metalled lanes and some muddy field paths. Around 600 feet (200m) total ascent and descent, including one long steep climb. Walking boots recommended

P Car park at the start

T BR station near the start

🍴 Pubs and cafés in Marple

panoramic view of the whole area.

Marple has an industrial history in which cotton manufacture and hat-making loom large. The town was very much shaped by an 18th-century entrepreneur, Samuel Oldknow, who began developing the cotton mills and related industries. His work is encountered more than once along the way.

ALONG THE CANAL

The route out of Marple follows the Peak Forest Canal. Mallard and tufted duck scavenge for food around the locks, begging titbits from passers-by. They are often accompanied by mute swans, which cruise regally up and down the canal between the narrowboats.

These locks are part of a famous flight of 16, which lift the canal 209 feet (63m). At between 13 and 14 feet (3.9 and 4.2m) each, they are the second deepest locks in the country. In places, they are so narrow that it is possible to leap from one side to the other, though each lock has a

THE WALK

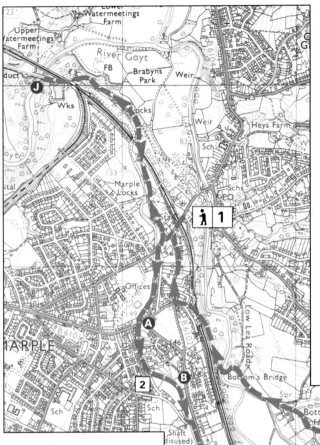

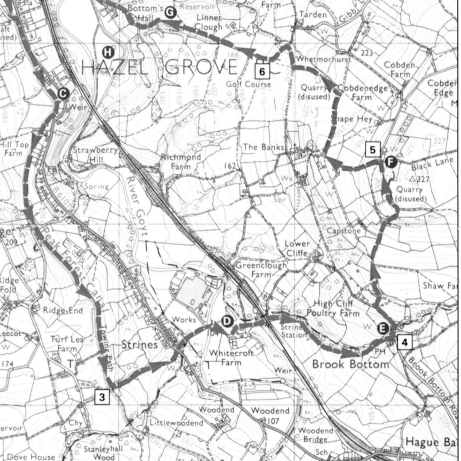

after passing a swing-bridge, take the cutting on your left down a steep embankment onto a track.

3 Bear left along this rough road and walk downhill towards the outskirts of Strines. Cross the busy road carefully and walk ahead along Station Road, past mills on your left and a large lake with an ornate dovecote **D** in the centre. The route rises towards Strines station. Take the left fork under a railway bridge, then turn immediately right, up a steep, well-defined path to Brook Bottom hamlet **E**.

4 Turn left along the road, then left again opposite a post-box along a signposted bridleway,

passing the Primitive Methodist chapel on your left. As the road levels out just before some farm buildings, take a footpath to your right over a wooden stile into a field. Ascend with the wall on your left for 50 yards (45m), then go through a squeeze-stile on your left. After about 20 paces, take the path diagonally up the slope, to the right of an agricultural building. From here, you can see the high-rise tower blocks of Manchester almost directly ahead. Follow the footpath up to the gate visible on the near horizon. Continue uphill through the next gate and along the tarmac lane, with the dry-stone wall on your right, to

MARPLE – BROOK BOTTOM – BOTTOM'S HALL

The walk begins in a free car park opposite Marple railway station, on the A626.

1 Turn left up the main road and cross the canal. Turn left down the towpath with the locks on your left. Go through a small tunnel under Posset Bridge **A**, and continue to a junction of two canals.

2 Take the left fork, waymarked 'Whaley Bridge', and walk along the right bank of the Peak Forest Canal. Just beyond the marina, look for the site of the lime-burning kilns **B** on the opposite bank. Cross the canal at bridge No. 19 and follow the towpath on the opposite bank for a further 1½ miles (2.4km) along the wooded canal **C**. About 150 yards (135m) another gate. Turn left along a lane past some stables, and along the summit up to a large wooden cross **F**.

▶ **5** Immediately after the cross, turn left down the minor road. About 100 yards (90m) after passing Bull Hill Farm, go through two wooden posts on your right onto the golf course. Continue along the top edge of the course, with the boundary wall to your right. Bear left at a small clump of birch trees, ignoring a minor path ahead that leads over a ditch to a wide stile. Veer right to walk along a stony track past the club car park, then turn sharp left, signposted to Linnet Clough scout camp.

▶ **6** Follow the path as it bears right and passes the scout camp. Continue down the bridleway, signposted 'Marple', descending gently. Continue past Bottom's Hall **G** and Mellor Mill, and Roman Lakes **H** on your left. At a crossroads, continue straight ahead along the minor road, which sweeps to the left and crosses the River Goyt. Follow the road over the railway just as it enters the tunnel. At a crossroads, turn right along Arkright Road. At its end, turn left then right down to the canal and the aqueduct **J**. Retrace your steps to the road and turn left downhill to the car park, where the walk started.

small bridge so that the operator can cross to open the gates.

The canal was opened in 1800, but the locks were not completed until 1804, owing to poor funding. In the meantime, a temporary tramway was built to carry goods from the bottom of the hill to what is now Top Lock.

At bridge No 18 **A**, the canal goes through a short tunnel, where the barges were walked through by leggers. The horses were unhitched and led through a horse-sized tunnel alongside. The bridge is known as Posset Bridge; the navvies' morale was flagging with the continuing delays, and Samuel Oldknow spurred them on to completion with supplies of ale posset (a drink made from alcohol and curdled milk) from the nearby Navigation Inn.

▲ *At Strines Print Works' reservoir is a dovecote with a weathervane. Behind it is one of the works' chimneys.*

Oldknow had sunk a great deal of money into the canal and was its chief promoter, relying on it for the transport of both raw materials and finished goods. He personally owned 15 barges, each of which cost the princely sum of £140 and could

◀ *At the hamlet of Brook Bottom the neatly maintained stone cottages are part of a Conservation Area. The return route to Marple runs for a stretch along a wooded track (below).*

carry 25 tons of produce.

His mills created a great deal of employment for women and children, whom he housed in the town. To provide work for their menfolk, he established a lime-burning concern, bringing the lime from Doveholes in Derbyshire. The limekilns **B** were designed to resemble a Gothic church so as not to spoil the view from Oldknow's house, Mellor Lodge.

The canal enters a wooded section **C**, where great spotted woodpeckers can be heard hammering in rapid bursts on the trunks of the mature trees. If you are fortunate, you may catch a glimpse of one as it darts through the woodland, its striking black and white plumage highlighted by a blood-red patch under its tail. In spring, nuthatches display by their chosen nesting holes, and are the natural

highlight of this section of the walk.

On the outskirts of Strines, the route crosses the valley of the River Goyt, passing a reservoir that originally served the nearby Strines Print Works. In the centre is an unusual dovecote **D**. This is now a listed building. A steep path leads to Brook Bottom **E**, a quaint little clump of cottages complete with pub and Primitive Methodist chapel. The whole hamlet is now registered as a Conservation Area.

HEAVENLY VIEWS

The style of the countryside changes dramatically as you climb Cobden Edge, on the borders of the Peak District. Ravens can be seen on these heights, persecuting any passing birds of prey unwise enough to try to hunt over their patch.

From a huge wooden cross **F**, erected in 1970 by a group of churches, there are splendid views of Kinder Scout and Chimley Churn in the Peak District to the east, over the sprawl of Manchester to the north-west, and the fertile Cheshire Plain to the south.

The route drops through a golf course back into the sphere of influence of Samuel Oldknow. Bottom's Hall **G**, the centre of his agricultural interests, was where he trained

◄Above the valley of the River Goyt the canal runs across an aqueduct alongside the railway viaduct.

▲*The millponds known as Roman Lakes once provided power for Mellor Mill but are now used for boating.*

apprentices in farming techniques. Poverty-stricken child workers were housed in an orphanage nearby.

Just beyond the Hall you will be able to see the Roman Lakes **H** through the trees. Originally millponds, they served Oldknow's giant Mellor Mill, which was opened in 1790. The mill made Oldknow the country's major producer of muslin, and continued to provide employment in the town until it was levelled by a fire in November 1892.

After recrossing the Goyt, a short jaunt leads along the canal to visit the remaining locks and the handsome Marple Aqueduct **J** (see box). Finally, you return to the start.

Marple Aqueduct

James Butterworth, the 19th-century historian, characterized Marple Aqueduct as 'one of the finest bridges in this or any of the neighbouring counties'. Even now, it is regarded as among the best features of the British canal system. Designed to carry the Peak Forest Canal 100 feet (30m) above the wooded valley of the River Goyt, it took seven years to build and was opened in 1800. Along the aqueduct's towpath there are four alcoves, one above each of the supporting columns. These allowed pedestrians to avoid the huge carthorses that pulled the barges along the canal.

The woods below the structure were used by bargemen as an

unofficial burial ground for any towing horses that died in harness. In later years, their bones were disinterred by other boatmen and sold to Strines Print Works for use in their dye-making processes.

Even in the last century, thousands of people enjoyed pleasure cruises across the aqueduct on public holidays, and it remains a major local attraction today. Later last century, however, the structure became overshadowed by the viaduct that carries the railway over the river. Though much larger than the aqueduct, it took only a year to build.

Built of brick and stone, Marple Aqueduct is still an imposing structure.

THURSTASTON HILL

A gentle walk to superb views of the surrounding countryside

Thurstaston Hill overlooks the magnificent Dee Estuary, a 30,000 acre (90 hectare) expanse of mudflats and salt marsh and a vital feeding ground for migrating birds. Thurstaston Hill itself, a heathland covered in gorse, heather and birch, is only 298 feet (90 metres) high, but it provides some of the most spectacular views in the Wirral.

COUNTRY PARK

Wirral Country Park was one of the first country parks to be established under the 1968 Countryside Act and follows the line of the old Hooton–West Kirby railway. Details of the area are provided at the Thurstaston Visitor Centre Ⓐ. Running through the park is the 12-mile (19-km) Wirral Way Ⓑ, which for over half its length runs directly parallel with the Dee Estuary.

The first section of the Hooton to Parkgate railway was opened in 1866 and it was later extended to West Kirby in 1868. The line was

▲ *The mudflats of the Dee Estuary make a perfect stopping-off place for migrating birds. The knot (inset) visits in autumn and spring on its way between Africa and the Arctic.*

originally built to serve the Neston colliery and there were plans to extend the line over the Dee Estuary to Flint on the Welsh coast. It was closed in 1956 and the track bed removed in 1962. Today the old line forms the backbone of the country park, but you can still see the old railway station platforms, bridges, railway cuttings and embankments.

At various places along the Wirral Way there are viewing points across the Dee Estuary Ⓒ. At low tide you can see the great expanse of mud and sandbanks, which in late summer and autumn become the home of great flocks of migrating birds including oyster catchers, shelducks, Canada geese and cormorants. During the winter months it is also an important wintering ground for waders and ducks.

VIEW OF WALES

Caldy Hill Ⓓ, a delightful sandstone ridge shaded by Scots pines, affords superb views over the estuary to Anglesey and on towards the Great Orme headland at Llandudno. On the summit of Thurstaston Hill stands a stone viewpoint Ⓔ depicting a map of the surrounding coastline. From here across the Estuary are Wales, the Clwydian

FACT FILE

✳	Thurstaston Country Park, Wirral
🗺	Pathfinder 738 (SJ 28/38), grid reference SJ 238834

miles 0 1 2 3 4 5 6 7 8 9 10 miles
kms 0 1 2 3 4 5 6 7 8 9 10 11 12 13 14 15 kms

◕	3 hours
▬	Easy walking along a disused railway and heathland paths
P	Thurstaston Visitor Centre
T / WC	Trains to West Kirby to join the walk 1 mile (1.6 km) along the Wirral Way at Stage 2
🍺	The Cottage Loaf pub at Thurstaston
🍴	Thurstaston Visitor Centre

THE WALK

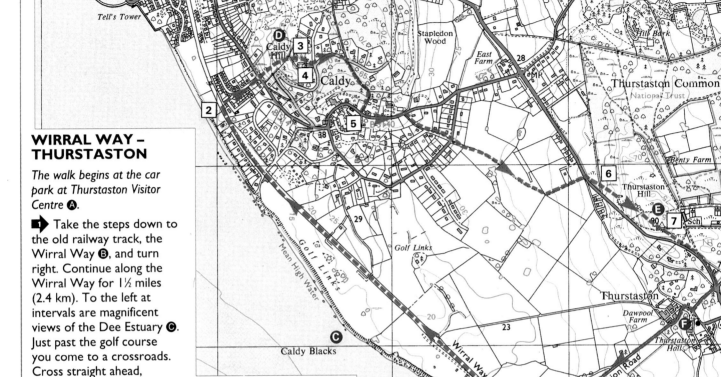

WIRRAL WAY – THURSTASTON

The walk begins at the car park at Thurstaston Visitor Centre Ⓐ.

1 Take the steps down to the old railway track, the Wirral Way Ⓑ, and turn right. Continue along the Wirral Way for 1½ miles (2.4 km). To the left at intervals are magnificent views of the Dee Estuary Ⓒ. Just past the golf course you come to a crossroads. Cross straight ahead, keeping Caldy car park on your right. About 150 yards (140 metres) on you come to another crossroads.

2 At the crossroads, turn right to a gate and continue up the road towards Caldy Hill Ⓓ. At the road junction, cross over to the gap in the fence almost directly opposite. Follow the small path up the hill towards a stony knoll and bench. Bear right to a gap in the stone wall.

3 Take the path on the left signed 'West Kirby', up the hill to a rocky pine-covered ridge.

4 Keep right and drop

down to a road junction. Walk straight on along Kings Drive to where a bridleway crosses the road. Take the walled track on the right and at the road bear right. Take the path on the right marked by a white metal sign to Thurstaston.

5 At the B5140 turn left, crossing the road at the T-junction to follow the waymarked track ahead. At the next road take the footpath opposite, to Thurstaston Common.

6 Follow the footpath through the heathland, keeping left and following the faint path ascending

gently between two rocky outcrops. Take the path on the left up to the ridge. At the ridge turn right to the viewpoint Ⓔ.

7 From the viewpoint walk to the white cairn and then take the path on the right. Ignore the first turning on the right, but take the second, which drops down to a car park. Turn left and go through a

gap in the fence signed picnic site, following a path that leads to a wooden stile and the road.

8 Turn right along the road past the Cottage Loaf Pub. At the crossroads turn right along the Station Road to Thurstaston village Ⓕ. At the village continue down Station Road to Thurstaston country park and the start of the walk.

Hills and Snowdonia's Carnedd Llwelyn, while across the Wirral Plain lies Liverpool. Further north, on a clear day it is sometimes possible to see Blackpool Tower and Black Combe in the Lake District.

Thurstaston village Ⓕ, built

◄The view from the top of Caldy Hill over the Dee Estuary to Clywd and the Welsh hills.

around a green, is now a conservation area. The records of the church go back to 1125 but the present red sandstone church is Victorian, built in splendid Gothic style in 1886. A plain stone tower of an early building still stands in the churchyard. Next to the church stands Thurstaston Hall. It is haunted by an old lady, a member of the Glegg family who once owned the Hall.

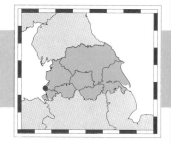

Seek out rare species where land and sea battle for supremacy

This walk explores the shifting coastline around Formby Point, where wind and waves have created an area of constant flux. No sooner do trees or grasses manage to colonize and stabilize the dunes, than a storm buries them all again beneath the sand. The efforts of man to reclaim land for agriculture have often met with the same fate.

RARE PLANTS

These natural processes, which can be seen in action at many points on the walk, have led to the creation of a variety of habitats that house some of Britain's rarer species.

The route begins by heading inland in search of unusual plants in a conifer woodland, where it follows the Woodlands Walk Trail ❶. During

▶ *On the Woodlands Walk Trail, the well-spaced trees let sunlight through, and there are some interesting plants.*

late spring and early summer, various species of helleborine can be found growing in the shade of the Scots, Corsican and Austrian pines, while late autumn brings out the fungi; waxcaps, russulas and earthstars are reasonably plentiful.

Fortunately for the wildlife — and for walkers — the trees are well spaced, letting sunlight penetrate to

▲*The trees of Gypsy Wood, now just gnarled stumps and bare branches, have been unable to survive exposure to the elements amid eroding dunes. Set back from the sea in mature dunes, you may find dune helleborine (inset) growing.*

FACT FILE

☀ Formby, 6 miles (9.6km) south-west of Southport

🗺 Pathfinder 710 (SD 20/30), grid reference SD 279082

miles 0 1 2 3 4 5 6 7 8 9 10 miles
kms 0 1 2 3 4 5 6 7 8 9 10 11 12 13 14 15 kms

◑ Allow 4 hours

▭ Level walking on sand, woodland paths and some metalled lanes

P On the wide grass verge at the start

T BR Freshfield Station

🍴 Pubs, cafés and restaurants in Formby

I National Trust information centre, Tel. (01704) 878591

THE WALK

FORMBY – FORMBY POINT

The walk starts on the grass verge just beyond the National Trust warden's office on the beach road from Freshfield station.

1 Walk back past the office and along the road to the level crossing at Freshfield railway station. Turn left down Montague Road. Keep ahead with the railway line to your left as the road becomes an unsurfaced track.

2 At a level crossing, turn left, carefully recrossing the railway, and go straight ahead across golf links. After ¼ mile (400m) turn right down a signposted footpath, and follow it past an information centre into conifer woods. Turn left down the signposted Woodlands Walk Trail **A**. Eventually, the Trail rejoins the original bridleway further north.

3 Turn right along the bridleway to return past the information centre to the Fisherman's Path **B**, and turn right. Follow the signs along this path for the beach, and continue ahead until you pass through a gap in the dunes onto the foreshore.

4 Turn left along the beach. You may wish to detour inland slightly, through the dunes, walking roughly parallel to the

shore. Continue for nearly 4 miles (6.4km), passing the remnants of Gypsy Wood **C** and Formby Point **D** until you reach the remains of the lifeboat station **E**.

5 Turn left through the dunes onto Lifeboat Road, a metalled road buried by sand. At a junction, turn left to walk along St Luke's Church Road. Just past the

church **F**, turn right into Edenhurst Drive, then left to head down Spruce Drive. Continue ahead along an alleyway between fences.

6 Turn right then soon left, and continue ahead along a broad footpath. Go ahead across the gorse-covered heathland, keeping close to the woods on your right, to reach pine woods. Take a route to the right of the pine woods, and along a hard track reinforced with brick. Walk straight across Blundell Avenue, making for the corner of the fence visible through the trees, and continue ahead on its left. At the end of the fence, go straight ahead along a well-defined footpath past the asparagus fields **G**, and through the Red Squirrel Reserve **H** back to your starting point.

---

the woodland floor. This encourages the flora and contributes to a pleasant, airy atmosphere very different from the dank gloom typically associated with conifer plantations.

FISHERMAN'S PATH

Dobson's Ride bridleway returns you from this unusual woodland onto the start of the aptly named Fisherman's Path **B**, originally trodden by anglers on bait-digging trips. On the right of the path is an excellent illustration of the different vegetation to be seen in the gradual transition from a beach to a soil-based environment.

First, in among the alien conifers, is a thick growth of silver birch, alder and sycamore. These trees could not grow on the sandhills, but rely on the soil laid down by the next zone of vegetation.

ADVANCING WOODLAND

Creeping willow, dewberry and various coarse grasses thrive on the fixed dunes. Their mat-like roots help lock the sand in place. When their leaves die, they rot down to

in off the Irish Sea on most days, whipping the dry sand into snakes that coil around your feet. If the tide is out, the sea is no more than a thin, silvery line on the horizon, but at high tide, the feet of the dunes are washed and licked by the waves.

GYPSY WOOD

Just as the trees attempt to colonize the dunes, so the woods have in several places along the shore been overcome by the sea and sand; Gypsy Wood ● is an example of this. As you approach Formby Point ●, look out for dark bands of humus, potent reminders of fixed dunes that existed when the zone of mobile dunes was on land now permanently below the sea.

▲ *There is a splendid contrast between the mature, stable dunes and the desert-like mobile dunes closer to the sea. Little remains of Britain's first lifeboat station (right), established in 1776.*

provide the rich humus vital to the advancing deciduous trees.

Closer still to the sea, marram grass, planted to stabilize the shifting sands of these mobile dunes, is about the only plant able to survive. Its roots go deep and can resist the winds that sweep away the sand. In very blowy conditions, a plume of sand trails from the crests of these dunes, to be caught and held by the fixed dunes further inland.

In between the dunes, boggy areas and pools of fresh water form. These wet slacks are vitally important environments, providing a habitat for many plants, including pyramidal and bee orchids.

NATTERJACK TOADS

Here, too, live natterjack toads, jocularly known as Lancashire nightingales, from their singing on muggy spring nights. Their high-pitched voices create a frenzied cacophony as the passionate males strive to attract mates. Natterjack toads have occupied these slacks for centuries, and are found almost nowhere else in Britain. They are strictly protected by law.

As you step out of the shelter of the towering dunes onto the usually deserted foreshore, you will probably feel the force responsible for sculpting them. A stiff breeze rushes

◀ *On the return leg of the walk, you come to St Luke's Church, known as 'the little church of the sandhills'. In its grounds, this dilapidated 'godstone' (below) supported a cross.*

Behind you, you may be able to pick out the Blackpool Tower across the Ribble Estuary, with the Cumbrian mountains behind. In the last century, local landowners tried to stabilize the dunes enough to allow a resort on the same scale as Blackpool to be developed at Formby, but the elements proved too powerful. If the horizon is clear and the sky bright, the peaks of Snowdonia will be clearly visible across the sea, and Anglesey clearly outlined ahead and to the right.

The beach walk leads eventually to the foundations of Britain's first lifeboat house **E**, built in 1776. The

The Red Squirrel Reserve

In 1967, the National Trust purchased some 400 acres (162 hectares) of dunes and woodlands around Formby Point. They have since turned the land into a popular tourist attraction, of which perhaps the major pull is the area west of Freshfield Station, where there is a small population of red squirrels. Unusually, the larger American grey squirrel, so common elsewhere, has not colonized this woodland.

The colony is not made up of native British red squirrels, however; these are a distinct subspecies, brought here from the Continent many years ago. Being much darker than the native species, they are instantly recognizable as introductions, though this in no way detracts from their charm as they willingly take food from the fingers of visitors.

A route called the Squirrel Walk has been marked out to take visitors around the sanctuary, and nuts purchased from the office at the entrance to the site keep the squirrels exceedingly well fed.

The red squirrel, with its bright eyes and bushy tail, is a popular Formby inhabitant.

▲*On the sandy heathland near the squirrel reserve, a mixture of trees provides a fine blend of foliage.*

boat served the local coastline until 1918, when the sands swept over the area and a team of horses was needed to drag the lifeboat to sea on wooden rollers.

At the top of Lifeboat Road, St Luke's Church **F** stands defiantly on a site previously occupied by a 12th-century chapel that was totally buried by the sands. Some artefacts recovered from it are now housed in the new 'little church of the sand-hills'. These include a Norman font and numerous tombstones and memorial tablets, including one to Richard Formby — an armour bear-er to Henry IV — whose family gave their name to the town.

In the graveyard are the old village stocks and the 'godstone', which held the market square cross before it fell into disrepair. The cross was made of wood sheathed in lead, and held a pool of vinegar in which residents left coins in return for goods in times of plague. The vinegar was believed to make the money safe to handle.

ASPARAGUS BEDS

The path back to the start leads through asparagus beds **G** reclaimed from the sandy landscape. Several huge beds of nettles nearby mark old tobacco leaf dumps, relics of the trade from America to nearby Liverpool. Another import from the Americas, the potato, was grown here for the first time in Britain. The walk ends with a stroll through the Red Squirrel Reserve **H** (see box).

INDEX

PICTURE CREDITS

All map artwork, MC Picture Library; Australian Overseas Information Service, London: 14bl; Reproduced by Kind Permission of Bamforth & Co: 46cl; H. J. Berry & Sons Ltd: 81br; Bradford Art Galleries & Museums: 37tl, 38bl; M. D. Boyes: 16br; Bridgeman: 32bl; Bruce Coleman: 25 inset, 49cc; BTA/ETB/SI: 16cl; Craven Photographics: 27tr; Christopher J. Duke: 25t, 26bl; Robert Eames: 19tr, 20bl; Derek Forss: 48bl, 81tr, 82bl, 82bc, 82br; Bob Gibbons: 55cr; N. K. Howarth/Brontë Parsonage Museum: 42tr; Images Colour Library: 43 inset, 44bl, 45cr, 46cr, 46bl, 96cl; Innes Photographic Library: 65bl, 69tr, 70cr, 70bl; Chris Kapolk: 42br; Kobal Collection: 24br; Frank Lane: 19cr, 61cc, 81cr; Manchester Public Libraries: 110cl; S&O Mathews: 68br; Sue Morris: 63tc, 63br, 64bc; National Maritime Museum, London: 16tc; National Portrait Gallery: 42tc; National Trust Photo Library: 13t, 120bl; Natural Image: 67cr; Nature Photographers: 13 inset, 33 inset, 63tl, 65cr, 77tc, 79cl, 83cl, 89cl, 119cr; NHPA: 11 inset, 17 inset, 21 inset, 29bc,37 inset, 39 inset, 57cr, 60bc, 71cl, 74cl, 75cr, 85tr, 101cc, 103cl, 115cr, 121tl, 124bl; Oldham Evening Chronicle: 114br; C. & H. S. Pellant 41br; Derek Pratt: 65tl, 66bc, 66br, 68tl, 68cr; Scotland in Focus: 97cl, 111cl; Roger Scruton: 17tc, 18bl; Sefton Photo Library: 119tr; Christine Simmons: 28cl, 28br; Jason Smalley: 33t, 33bl, 35cr, 36tr, 36cl, 36br, 53tr, 54bl, 71t, 73tl, 73tr, 73bc, 73cr, 74tl, 74bl, 75t, 76cl, 76br, 83tl, 84br, 85tl, 86bl, 87bc, 88tr, 88cl, 88br, 89tl, 89br, 91tl, 91cl, 91br, 92tr, 92bl, 97tl, 97br, 98bl, 99tr, 99br, 100tr, 100cl, 100br, 101t, 102cl, 102br, 103tl, 105cr, 106cl, 106cb, 115t, 115bl, 117tr, 117bl, 117br, 118tr, 118cl, 118br,121t, 121bc, 123tl, 123cr, 123bc, 123br, 124tr; Spectrum: 45tr; Swift Picture Library: 27 inset, 47 inset, 53cr, 93bc, 105cr, 107cr; Simon Warner: 12bl, 13br, 14bc, 15br, 21t, 21br, 23tl, 23cr, 23bc, 29tr, 31tl, 31cr, 31bl, 32tr, 32cl, 39tr, 39br, 40bl, 42cl, 42bl, 47tl, 48br, 49tr, 50bl, 51cl, 51br, 52tr, 52bl, 77t, 77bl, 78bl, 79tl, 79br; John Watney: 11tr, bl, br; Mike Williams: 55tr, 55bl, 56br, 57t, 57bl, 59tl, 59bl, 59br, 60tl, 60cr, 60bc, 61tr, 93cl, 95tl, 95cl, 95tr, 95br, 96tr, 96br, 107cl, 109cl, 109cr, 109br, 110tr, 110cr, 111tl, 111br, 112bl, 113bl, 113br, 114tr, 114cl.